Reflections from Afar

Unexpected Blessings for Those Who "Have"
from Those Who Don't

By Cory Trenda

Editorial director: Milana McLead
Editor-in-chief: Jane Sutton-Redner
Project editor: Laurie Delgatto
Copyediting and design: Creative Solutions, World Vision U.S.
Sales and distribution manager: Jojo Palmer

Printed in the United States of America

ISBN 978-09827162-2-9

At the author's request, all royalties due to the author will benefit
World Vision's work with children in need.

Endorsements

Cory was in the room when I heard God's call to become an HIV/AIDS advocate. He took me to Africa and invited me to enter into the sufferings of widows, orphans, and vulnerable children. My wobbly first steps were shepherded by Cory. I recognized that he has a unique way of seeing life through spiritual eyes, and he is able to transform what he sees into stirring words that paint pictures of the life we share in common with brothers and sisters around the world.

—Kay Warren, co-founder of Saddleback Church in Lake Forest, CA, and founder of Saddleback's HIV/AIDS Initiative

Cory Trenda brings us a compelling message with genuine honesty. He reminds us that we all lack in some areas of life; hence giving and receiving from each other is the greatest gift. I consider Cory a personal friend, having known and worked with him for several years, and through his heartfelt writing, I now realize what a humble servant and a great advocate for the poor and forgotten we have in our midst. His is a voice to be reckoned with, both for those who "have" and those who "have not." This book is a must-read.

—Princess Kasune Zulu, author of Warrior Princess, *global HIV and AIDS advocate, and founder of Fountain of Life, a charitable organization benefiting children orphaned by AIDS in Zambia*

Reflections from Afar is for those who grapple with what it means to be a person of faith in the midst of seemingly intractable global disparities between the "haves" and the "have-nots." Without romanticizing or spiritualizing the plight of those living in impoverished conditions, or wallowing in the guilt of living with plenty, Cory humbly and honestly shares journeys on which he encounters the hope of the kingdom in the most seemingly unlikely places and people. *Reflections* reminds us that the kingdom is closer than we think.

    —***Michael Mata***, *community transformation specialist and adjunct professor at Claremont School of Theology and Fuller Seminary*

In these honest reflections and penetrating stories, Cory allows us to share his long journey of moving between the worlds of America's affluence and global poverty, drawing us into the depths of human suffering and the impact of Christian response. This is a rare glimpse into the heart and mind of one who has spent much of his life discovering, and helping others to discover, the signs of hope in the midst of desperate global poverty. My heart, mind, and memories were deeply touched and stretched. Insightful and stirring.

    —***Rev. Dr. Roberta Hestenes***, *former president of Eastern College/ University, faculty member at Fuller Seminary, and senior pastor at Solana Beach Presbyterian Church, Solana Beach, CA*

With artfully chosen words, the author transports me to places I've never been. I can visualize the people he's met and the suffering he's seen. And I will not forget the heart-expanding lessons he's learned, often from those who suffer the most, often through painful evaluation of his own shortcomings. I know people whose hearts harden toward God because of "all the suffering He allows in the world." How helpful it might be for those hard hearts to caravan with Cory and to see with him how a loving God, aided by His loving emissaries, is bringing hope and life to even the darkest corners of our world.

—*Tom Theriault, Outreach Pastor, Solana Beach Presbyterian Church, Solana Beach, CA*

A lovely tapestry of stories of generosity from one who intersects with the poor and the rich, the giver and the recipient.

—*Dave Gibbons, pastor and author of* The Monkey and the Fish: Liquid Leadership for a Third-Culture Church

This is a book that will warm your heart and build your faith. From the front lines of World Vision's ministry among the poor, the author's humble listening is met by the teaching of the poor and God's Holy Spirit. This book is perfect for [those] who want to open themselves to a different world, full of pain and poverty but also of hope and wisdom.

—*Bryant L. Myers, Ph.D., Professor of International Development, School of Intercultural Studies, Fuller Theological Seminary*

Reflections from Afar is a journey into the hearts and lives of the vulnerable and marginalized among us. Voicing their stories with raw honesty and a teachable spirit, Cory Trenda leads us along a spiritual pathway of discovery, giving us an opportunity to cross the divide and to be present with wide-open hearts. This is a must-read for everyone concerned with God's heart for our world.

> —**Rev. Canon Paul-Gordon Chandler**, *author, Episcopal priest, and interfaith advocate and Rector of St. John's Church, Cairo, Egypt*

The poignant word-pictures in *Reflections from Afar* penetrate the soul. Cory takes us into places of desolation and gives us eyes to behold amazing beauty among the poor. These glimpses of the kingdom inspire and convict.

> —**Robert (Bob) Lupton, Ph.D.**, *president of FCS Urban Ministries, Atlanta, GA*

Cory Trenda has a passionate heart for God and a compassionate heart for both the world generally and the poor specifically. His sensitively and beautifully written reflections will reach into your soul, challenge your mind, wrench at your heart, and move your will to both prayer and action.

> —**Michael Cassidy**, *founder, African Enterprise, Pietermaritzburg, South Africa*

Cory Trenda is an authentic soul—honest, introspective, and caring. His life's journey exposes him every day to the glaring contrasts between "rich" and "poor." This book reveals an understanding that will benefit us all. In the overwhelming world of global poverty, Cory shows us that the richest abundance of our most important human qualities—selfless compassion, enduring optimism, and courageous determination—can be found in the darkest and most unexpected places. This book will touch your heart and challenge your perspective on life.

—*Bruce Krysiak, chairman of the board of Susser Holdings, Quantum Health, LaDove Inc., and Bristol Farms; former President of Toys"R"Us and Dollar General*

Cory introduces us to people we normally look past . . . the beggar woman in Chennai, the woman collecting trash in a food court, the homeless woman with HIV in Ethiopia . . . and in so doing, he reveals something of ourselves and of God.

—*Cary Paine, Executive Director, The Stewardship Foundation*

Reflections from Afar offers a simple yet profound way for readers to enter into issues of poverty and misery, yet come through refreshed and encouraged. This book is an invitation to see our shared humanity and to see the poor and vulnerable through the eyes of a loving God.

—*Rich Stearns, president of World Vision U.S.*

Acknowledgments

My deep appreciation goes to Mark Archibald, Jeff Witten, Karey Sabol, and my wife, Janet, who faithfully plodded through drafts of most of these entries over the past few years as I navigated various ramblings and rants, as well as to the readers who have endured some of these via e-mail and greatly encouraged my sometimes-painful honesty along the way.

Thanks also to Milana McLead and her team at World Vision Resources for having a vision to publish these reflections to reach a wider audience.

Most of all, I'm thankful to the desperately poor whom I have met, who have inspired me beyond all writing of it and who continue to teach me more and more about Jesus and His call on my life. This book is humbly dedicated to them.

Table of Contents

Preface

Afar. It's a mythical state of mind, and it's an actual place.

Afar is a large region in northeastern Ethiopia, near the Djibouti border, where I've traveled several times for World Vision, the large Christian humanitarian organization for whom I work. The Afar region is home to the famous skeleton Lucy, considered by some to be the world's first human, and home to the Danakil Desert, which *National Geographic* recently called "The Cruelest Place on Earth." Afar is such an appropriate name for this remote area and its self-described "forgotten people"; it's one of those places of which it can be said, "It's not the end of the earth, but you can see it from there."

On one of my visits there, we took a Sunday afternoon drive to see a nearby lake. Afterward, as we walked up a hot, dusty trail to get back to our vehicle, we saw six Afar men standing nearby. We had just heard that a sick woman had been carried across the lake on a makeshift raft. As we got closer, we saw the young woman lying under the shade of a tree, ill and still, on a woven mat with two heavy poles protruding from the ends. These six men had carried her all the way to the lake on this mat and then managed to ferry her across. Yet they were still 20 miles from the only clinic where she could get help that day, with no way to reach it before it would close.

We talked with the local staff who were hosting us: "Is there anything we can do?" They told us ominously that some time ago, staff had given a ride to someone who was sick with hepatitis. Soon, everyone who had been in that vehicle developed hepatitis and had been unable to do their important work for many days. So this was not something to consider lightly!

But because of her obvious need (and my equally obvious

consternation, I suppose), the decision was made for a couple of the local staff and me to risk driving the young woman and two of her carriers to the clinic, though they insisted I sit up front, further from the sick woman. Meanwhile, her other attendants had to simply follow on foot.

We drove to the clinic, each lost in our own thoughts—no doubt praying for our personal protection along the way, as well. Eventually, we all prayed together for God's healing for this Muslim woman, now limp against her husband's shoulder.

Then it happened: For a fleeting moment, I silently conducted my own award ceremony and pinned a little badge of pride on my chest for what we were doing and how I'd helped organize it. I could see myself telling my wife and others the story of how we'd helped serve—and maybe even save—this woman, despite the cost and risk to ourselves.

Immediately, I found myself choking back sobs. What did I know of the cost of servanthood? Traveling mile after dusty mile, yet in our comfortable vehicle, drove home the measure of true sacrifice amid the harsh environment that these people live in every day. The Afar men had carried the woman on a mat, by hand and foot, fully expecting to walk the entire journey, until God blessed them in the form of our God-orchestrated arrival. Our little shuttle service was nothing compared to their service—days and miles of toil and risk, willingly undertaken on her behalf.

And of course, sitting up front in the vehicle (albeit under protest), I was at decidedly less risk than my colleagues sitting near her. If King David had it right when he refused to offer a sacrifice that didn't cost him anything—that the value of an offering to God is in direct proportion to what it costs the giver—then I had missed the point completely.

I took off my little badge, repented, and gazed straight ahead from behind the tears in my eyes, reflecting on the biblical lesson of costly sacrifice that I was learning from the example of these servants of Allah.

How much I still have to learn from "others."

Afar is not just a region in Ethiopia; it's also a state of mind, a mythic place of mystery where the "others" live—those who are different, unknown. I could say afar is the opposite of where I am, a place distant, an epic journey, a state so foreign as to be almost beyond my comprehension.

Yet in my work, I've had the privilege of traveling "afar" to many parts of our world—not often to the usual tourist stops (which I'd love to see someday), but rather to impoverished rural villages and slums not shown on most maps or known to tour guides. It's in these places of mystery (to an American suburbanite like me) where I've had deep encounters: with the poor, with Jesus, and with myself.

The wise men "traveled afar," according to the Christmas carol. No one is sure where "afar" was. Still, we know they came to pay homage, bearing precious gifts from their homelands and propelled by a unique—perhaps divine—knowledge that an exceptional King had been born, a knowledge that shocked those under whose very noses the event had occurred.

Precious gifts still come from afar. For me, traveling afar—and near—has given me new eyes to see my own reality very differently. New ears to hear very differently the words of the Shepherd of Judea and His call on my life. And new resolve to pay homage with my choices, as I live out my commitment to Jesus and His kingdom's reign in my everyday life.

Throughout my journey, I've been building altars and dropping breadcrumbs in the form of reflections, which I send out to friends. This book is a compilation of some of my reflections on living life as a middle-class American in light of the encounters I've had and the lessons I'm learning from the "others" from afar.

I invite you to join the caravan as we journey together to find the King and glimpse signs of His coming kingdom.

—Cory Trenda
September 2010

Uncomfortable Generosity

Last Saturday we met my son and grandkids to celebrate the twins' birthday. As we sat outside at a multi-restaurant food court, a Hispanic employee in her tidy uniform came by, picking up trash with a trigger-handled pole that had rubber-lipped pincers on the end. I marveled that she could pick up the tiniest piece of straw wrapper without stooping down. Several times, I commented with a "Wow!" on what a wonderful tool it was. "I want one of those!" I affirmed with a smile to this pleasant-faced, middle-aged woman. I spoke respectfully, concerned that she not mistake my friendliness for condescension.

She smiled, nodded, and moved on to pick up trash in other areas.

Half an hour later she was back again with her fancy tool—this time with an identical one still in the packaging, which she thrust into my hand, speaking a few words in Spanish that I didn't understand. I assumed at first that she wanted to show me what the package looked like so I could go buy one myself, or that maybe she would let me try out the new one. She, however, didn't understand my words either and apparently thought I wanted her to unwrap the new one for me, which she carefully did. Then she firmly handed it back to me.

I got up and animatedly tried it out—it worked great! I was ready to hand it back but when I turned around, she was gone. Nowhere to be found.

I kept looking around, trying to decide how to appropriately respond. Could I pay her? If so, how much? But no, that would cheapen her graciousness.

Maybe there was something I could give her in return? I quickly tried to assess my assets at hand to find something commensurate with her kindness. But my efforts were futile. She never came back.

Did she give away her employer's possession? Would it put her job at risk? What if someone saw her do it?

All the while, my son was sitting back, assuring me I should simply accept the gift and relax—the same advice I always give to travelers on international trips to visit World Vision projects when one of them is overwhelmed with the generosity of the poor. I self-assuredly spout off about leaning in, about accepting, as though I'm the expert. But subconsciously I comfort myself with a feeling that part of the generosity shown to visitors is actually in thanks to my organization and the impact our programs have already had on the life of this poor person, that the visitor simply represents all donors and is thereby the lucky, albeit uncomfortable, recipient.

I'm full of garbage.

Here was no such substitutionary reciprocity, no gratitude for the impact of some blessing that I am counted as representing. Just kindness. Raw generosity.

Maybe the pincer tool was hers to give, maybe not. Even if she hadn't been the purchaser, she could be charged for it, or possibly fired for giving it away. Yet she wasn't clandestine about the gift; the people at the adjacent tables all watched our animated conversation. (Although perhaps that's why she disappeared again so quickly.)

Her gracious, simple generosity consumed my thoughts for the rest of the birthday party.

How does one account for the amazing generosity of the poor in many cultures? How can I claim to be a person who promotes and inspires generosity in others yet not even know how to accept the smallest, purest gesture of it?

A generous donor recently said to me (though it was clear he was mildly scolding himself), "Don't thank me for donating, Cory. Let's face it: I'm not giving out of my hardship, but out of my abundance.

My giving doesn't really impact my lifestyle, and almost everyone else you work with is in the same situation."

We who are not poor may never understand the ethos of those who are, and why they can be so unabashedly generous. That's why the story of the poor widow who put a mere pittance in the temple treasury (Mark 12:42) has made the papers for 2,000 years and continues to bother us. Because she gave everything she had. Who would do that? It doesn't make any earthly sense.

And yet there it is. The act itself screams for our attention. It slams up against our own calculations and says, "There is another way—a way of freedom and trust."

Of course, we may spiritualize the story and think it's all about donating money for the church or other official nonprofit organizations. But then what do we say about the more than 73,000 local volunteers around the world, trained and organized by World Vision but mustered by their own compassion and commitment, who are caring for those sick and dying of HIV and AIDS in their midst? They not only don't get paid, but they share of their own families' meager food supplies to feed the sick; use their own money to buy needed supplies; and care for children who have been orphaned, either in their own homes or with financial support. It makes me bow my head in honor to recall how these humble bands of 10 to 12 villagers each—most of them women—minister to their neighbors from their own poverty.

When those memories and the realities behind them slam into me, I realize again how little I understand about giving, and how much we've lost as we've gained material comfort.

Tim Dearborn of World Vision's Christian Commitment team, an often-prophetic voice among us, recently said, "Our job is to connect those who are rich in commodities with those who are rich in community." Isn't that beautiful?

Who's poor? Who's rich? We all are.
What we have, they need. Sometimes desperately.
What they have, we need. Just as desperately.

Where There Is Hope

Yes, I saw the new latrine. I saw the newly tarpapered roof, too. Just like my grandfather used to hammer on his little boathouse at the lake cottage 50 years ago. Except that this entire home was half the size of that one-boat shed.

These were some of the achingly simple accomplishments proudly displayed by the residents of Las Palmas, a desperately poor *colonia* on the outskirts of Tijuana, Mexico. I live and work less than 100 miles from the U.S.-Mexico border in Orange County, California, serving World Vision's major contributors who live in this southwestern-most corner of America. "Sea to shining sea" stops right here. And on the other side of the border, at least in the areas we visited, it's another world altogether.

I can drive to the border crossing, meet local staff who pause their critical work to graciously serve as our hosts, experience the developing world in the squatter slums where World Vision operates, and then have dinner at home and sleep in my own bed. It's supremely convenient, though culture shock is my constant companion.

I took a group of donors across the border yesterday to see World Vision's projects among the poorest communities. Today I'm exhausted. A couple times the fatigue caught up with me; I felt a nagging fear that the progress we'd seen was all just cheery window dressing on a shipwreck. I wished that I could more easily weep for the people of Las Palmas. I wished that I could convince God to fix their world.

Yesterday I played the role I love: energetic leader of our visiting group. I asked tons of questions, helped everyone understand what was happening and what was being discussed, and encouraged the residents in their valiant efforts to heave off their crushing poverty—poverty that's like a huge boulder they must push up the steep, trash-speckled hills.

We had to take the longer way into the community, down a steep incline, because of huge ruts from the winter rains that wreck the canyon road. I remembered the time a couple years ago when I visited a nearby community on a different garbage-strewn hill. It had rained for four or five days. I vividly recall walking through one proud woman's home to see her new latrine out back. Her house-of-cards dwelling had a dirt floor. As we walked through the house we followed the damp tracks where rivulets of water had run downhill during the rains. The tracks took us all the way to the back kitchen wall, where a small, framed poem hung. In Spanish, it read:

Where there is Faith there is Hope
Where there is Hope there is Peace
Where there is Peace there is God
Where there is God nothing is missing

Wow!

We definitely saw powerful signs of hope yesterday—a great many of them in the eyes of the community members. But for every one of those signs, we saw 20 signs of despair: kids not attending school, horrid living conditions, old outhouses that fill with rain and flood the area with their disease-infested contents.

All I can tell myself with honesty is this: It's better than it was when I was here three years ago. And *they* are holding onto that truth.

I guess that's the way it is with hope. Hope itself is the very evidence that things are, in fact, *not yet seen*. The presence of hope means the absence of what's hoped for. People in these conditions get many opportunities to practice hope. I could take a master's-level course in hope from them.

If it's true that "Where there is faith, there is hope," then Jesus' words about needing faith only the size of a mustard seed to move mountains is indeed good news to the poor.

He used the same analogy in a kingdom parable: "'The kingdom of heaven is like a mustard seed, which a man took and planted in his field. Though it is the smallest of all your seeds, yet when it grows, it is the largest of garden plants and becomes a tree, so that the birds of the air come and perch in its branches'" (Matthew 13:31-32).

I don't like it when writers throw out a Scripture verse to cover an unsightly corpse with a happy-ever-after eulogy, and I won't do that here. But I'll say this: For him who has eyes to see, there are new branches on that mustard seedling of hope in Las Palmas—maybe even some buds.

We were told that there is no longer a need for World Vision to assist in providing latrines. We've helped the community make their voices heard; they've lobbied the city so successfully that sanitation lines (a distant dream three years ago) are nearly complete. Running water comes to some homes and even to some toilets. The steep road we drove yesterday was unnavigable last time, but today it's paved. The residents are convincing the city that they are a community deserving of respect: "Come with plowshares to help us, not demolition equipment to destroy us!" It's right to tap into a community's own resources—and hope—rather than bringing those in from outside.

The residents all came together to build a new cinder-block community center dug into the hillside. No electric lights or anything else yet, but we sat in the building shell and heard 20 volunteer leaders talk with pride and show us photos. Their amazing success in mobilizing the 600 families in this community—many of whom now believe there is reason to hope—was at least as important as the building itself.

We met Claudia, a microcredit borrower who was cheated out of her home but is still working, still saving. When we asked, "How have you seen God at work in your group?" Claudia, a strong Christian, was the first to respond, speaking with moist eyes of God's mercy and His sustaining grace in her life.

One of the community bank microcredit groups was named "Hope for the Future." We visited the little *tienda* (shop) run by the group's president, Guadalupe. She lives on her own, so this new business is her lifeline. When asked what she likes most about running a business, she answered, "I'm my own boss now; I don't have to do what someone else says," with passion that hinted of a darker meaning.

So what heights of freedom does this give Guadalupe? She now works from 7 a.m. until 9 p.m., seven days a week. We asked if she's unable to go to church due to her demanding schedule. She answered that sometimes she'll leave her brother (who helps as her security guard) at the store so she can attend weekday services. Finally we asked about her hopes for the future. By this point in her story I think all of us—even Guadalupe—were aware that the mountain she has to climb is higher than the daunting hills cradling Las Palmas. Her eyes were tinged red, but with determination she told us of her commitment to make her business succeed and her dream to become economically self-sufficient.

Signs of faith. Signs of hope. Signs of the planted and growing mustard seed, the kingdom of heaven.

Bob Pierce founded World Vision with a prayer: "Let my heart be broken with the things that break the heart of God." One of yesterday's visitors e-mailed me: "I didn't sleep well last night, Cory. All those faces and stories were so prominent in my mind and heart." I was glad to hear it. Another seed planted. Another sign of the kingdom.

Life With Hindrances

I'm sitting in the small oak grove in the ravine near my home, reminded of the saying, "A beautiful young person is an accident of nature. A beautiful old person is a work of art." For these trees, life is all about adapting to hindrances and flourishing anyway. They really can't do a single thing about the hindrances. It all comes down to shade, brush, light, disease, and location, location, location. The trees are planted where they are and that's where they will always be. Their only option is to do their best, even with broken limbs, exposed roots, and other trees blocking the light.

The beauty lies in their struggle to live and flourish:

- A thick stump—the debris of a calamitous crash rotting into fertilizer around it—sprouts a lovely halo of new growth above its decapitated trunk.
- A twisted, bent tree near the bank appears totally dead on one side but the other side is full of leaves shading the creek.

Not "perfection" beauty, but the beauty that is life—any way we can manage it.

These freakish trees are rarely erect and nowhere near perfect or symmetrical. Lurching to one side or another to grab sunlight, they form a lovely canopy of checkered shade and speckled light, offering a sanctuary of crunching leaves on which to sit, meditate, and write while the breeze blows through their tops and more debris wafts down around me—birds and creek the only sounds. A holy place. A mountain cathedral.

My mind shifts easily to the poor whom I've met around the world and to the beauty brought about by their many debilitating hindrances. I think of the "imperfect" bodies, stunted growth, bent shapes. Of Olipa in Malawi and her triangular neck that was weathered like saddle leather from her lifelong chores of carrying water and who-knows-what-else on her head. Of the deformed, scarred, unshod feet in every place, worn from life and infection and poorly healed injuries. Of gnarled fingers and backs and bony structures: all bent, misshapen, worn down.

And yet there is life, survival, a life-affirming passion to thrive despite difficulty. Often with a checkerboard smile. To adapt, to lean toward the light, to send a new shoot jutting out to capture energy. It's beautiful—a thing to behold, appreciate, and respect despite its "imperfection."

Oh, to understand this, Lord. On one hand, I need to embrace the hindrances around me. I need to learn from the trees how to accept and adjust to the things I cannot change. It's not a very American attitude, but it's appropriate more often than I've appropriated it.

On the other hand, is it right to apply the same attitude of acceptance to the plight of others, at least when the ability to make a difference is in my power (a phrase that trees would never consider)? It doesn't seem proper to apply the same lesson. Nor biblical.

The biblical perspective advocates greater equality. The apostle Paul says it well: "Our desire is not that others might be relieved while you are hard pressed, but that there might be equality. At the present time your plenty will supply what they need, so that in turn their plenty will supply what you need. Then there will be equality, as it is written: 'He who gathered much did not have too much, and he who gathered little did not have too little'" (2 Corinthians 8:13-15).

Even though greater acceptance makes sense when relating to my own difficulties, the gospel does not call us to accept as unchangeable fact the suffering of others, even though we appreciate their beauty as survivors of a life with hindrances.

In the same grove near my home is a grassy clearing where one mighty oak stands unobstructed, whole, symmetrical. Perfect. And an accident of nature. After all, what did that tree do to bring this about? One acorn rolled down the hillside into the clearing, where it doesn't have to vie for light or space with anything else, unlike all the other "hindered" trees.

Truly, a beautiful, unhindered life, while beautiful, is an accident of nature. A beautiful life with hindrances is a work of art.

The Ministry of Touch, Tears, and Blood

On a trip to Ethiopia, a group of donors and I visited Afar. Among many encouraging and meaningful visits, one encounter was especially powerful and unexpected.

Rather than drive off as usual through the dust and sand to some rural project site, we stayed right in town. Just after we arrived, our hosts took us to a humble community center and ushered us into a small, dimly lit room. When our eyes adjusted, we saw that on one side, 50 or more gaunt, weak-looking adults sat shoulder-to-shoulder. We learned that this was the support group for people living with HIV and AIDS. It took us a moment to recover; this visit was a surprise. But once we got our bearings, one of us, then another, and soon all of us stepped forward to shake hands with the people on the front row. We pushed our chairs forward so we could be close to them and listen to their stories. "I thank God for this project. Now that I'm on medicines, I've regained 30 pounds!" "We were supposed to die. This project is giving us our lives back!" "After my family threw me out of the house, I was able to rent a room in another house thanks to the $6 monthly rental support I receive."

We asked others how their families had responded when the members learned they were HIV-positive. That's when the crowded room became a holy sanctuary. One by one, reluctantly at first, they feebly stood and spoke:

"My family won't touch me anymore. They won't let me eat from the same dish. I'm an outcast."

"I had to leave home and rent a room in another house. After awhile the family there wouldn't let me use the toilet. They finally made me sleep outside."

A woman stood and explained with tears, "Last night I was thrown out of my house. What will I do now?"

Another told of disclosing her HIV status to her husband. To calm her fear of rejection and abandonment, he bravely promised not to throw her out of the house. Instead (due to his lack of understanding of AIDS prevention), he told her that the family would simply "all die together." She wept as she explained that now her husband and son must also be tested, pouring out her fear that they may also receive the dreaded diagnosis.

A young family of three was there: The husband, wife, and 6-year-old son all were HIV-positive.

Many others poured out heartrending stories of struggling with the reality of HIV and AIDS. It was overwhelming. As their wretched reality sunk in, one of our team members began to cry silently. Some of the ladies in the front row of the support group saw his tears streaming down, and they too began to weep. A holy connection was made as we shared their pain.

At one point our hosts told us that we needed to leave to stay on schedule, but it was clear in that moment that there was no more important thing we could do than to simply stay and listen to these people—outcasts who were so grateful to have someone take an interest in their suffering.

That evening as we debriefed, I told the group I'd had trouble concentrating the rest of the day. Stew, the one who had ministered with his tears, told us that when we arrived at our next stop he was again consumed by the experience and started to choke up. Embarrassed, he tried to surreptitiously wipe his nose on his sleeve. His arm came away striped with blood; his nose had started to bleed. He ducked behind one of the vehicles to compose himself but felt increasingly overwhelmed. Just then, one of the Ethiopian staff came over to comfort him. The man wiped the blood and tears off Stew's face and helped him clean up. What a powerful contrast to the experience of those living with HIV and AIDS, whose families wouldn't touch them anymore and were afraid of their blood and bodily fluids. Stew felt incredible compassion wash over him as this young staff person beautifully and tenderly ministered to him in his vulnerability and weakness.

In many ways this same ministry, the ministry of touch, of tears, and of blood, is the ministry to which we are all called. It is the way Jesus ministered in His compassionate identification with the broken and suffering. He came, He touched, He wept, and He bled.

And He calls us to do the same. It is the way of the cross.

Hungry Hearts

On my most recent trip to Ethiopia, Jen, the youngest traveler in our group, showed us the power of unrestrained compassion.

One evening, a few of us visited an impoverished widow who had set up a sewing business outside her front door. It was the quintessential African entrepreneur photo-op: a hardworking tailor sitting at her treadle sewing machine, colorful fabrics hanging on the wall behind her, tween daughter at her side. But as we chatted, it became apparent that something was missing. When I asked about her dreams for her business, she replied with dull eyes that she wanted to expand her offerings, but she wasn't able to save any money to increase her inventory. Her household expenses took up everything she made. She lacked the usual smile and can-do attitude of most microentrepreneurs I'd met. We shook hands and did our best to encourage her despite her challenges. As we drove away, the staff told us she was living with HIV.

Later that evening I confirmed what I had suspected—this was the first time Jen and the other members of the group had shaken the hand of an HIV-positive person. I sensed that questions about their exposure to germs and viruses were running through their minds. Would they have touched her had they known her HIV status in advance? I told the group it was a healthy warm-up to our first stop the coming morning: a visit to the HIV-positive support group I'd met three years earlier. I didn't go into detail, but told them it had been a powerful encounter.

At the meeting with the HIV support group the next day, we sat in a circle with 40 or so group members, our backs against the wall of a round, plastered building with a thatched roof. I purposely shook lots of hands as we entered and sat between two members of the support group. But the rest of the team was fairly reserved.

I looked around for the faces of the support group members I'd photographed three years ago. I recognized precious few.

Yet their stories and their pain were similar. In Ethiopia, people with HIV and AIDS are often shunned, feared, and treated much like lepers were in Jesus' day. I listened carefully, and this time I actually found slight reasons for hope. A housekeeper told us that since she'd contracted HIV her job duties had changed (she is no longer allowed to use her employer's dishes nor prepare food for the family), but she hadn't lost her position. That represents measurable progress in the reduction of stigma and fear in that community. Another woman said she was able to rent a room in someone else's home even though she had HIV.

Despite these improvements, it was clear that the sting of being considered "unclean" was viscerally just as painful to this cohort as it had been to the earlier group.

The group has now created their own home-based care team of 10 members. This heroic team visits the sick who are "on bed," bathes them, washes their clothes and bedding, and performs other acts of compassion and service that their own families are unwilling to perform. In one especially sad vignette, the leader explained that often families won't even bathe the dead to prepare them for burial according to their custom. The home-based care team gives those who die as a result of AIDS the dignity of a proper washing and burial. "We must bury our own," the leader told us, with a mixture of shame and defiance that I'll never fully fathom.

After awhile, these stories became a battering ram pounding at my heart. I was among the transgressors recently enough, the fearful whose reservations speak rejection to the sick and dying—the ones who most need compassion and care. Societal change is excruciatingly slow, especially when death for many may be only a few years away, or less. My heart was sick.

It was time to wrap up and leave, but I asked if I could first address the group. I felt led to share Stew's story of "touch, tears, and blood" from our visit three years earlier. As I did, a few nodded in remembrance. I told how Stew wept for the pain this group feels, and how the World Vision staff worker had wiped away his tears and blood. I could feel the yearning these people all had to be touched and ministered to in such a way. How could they help but think, "Well, that's fine for your HIV-free American friend, but no one will ever treat me that way save perhaps the home-based care team, our 'fellowship of the damned.'"

I realized I had nothing to say. Nothing would be gained by assuring them everything will be all right or that God loves them equally. They were on one side of the chasm and I was on the other. My empty reassurances would simply fall into the divide that separated us. All I could do was acknowledge their pain and loneliness. With a quivering voice, I told them how very sorry I was that they are treated so shamefully. I felt their pain deeply and could only agree with them how much we all ache for human touch, ache to be treated as Stew had been.

I asked if we could join hands so that I might pray for the group. I'm proud to say that at this point all of our team reached out their hands without reservation and left them open. Many of those with HIV hesitated to touch us, perhaps because they were so accustomed to "knowing their place." But one by one, almost every hand clasped another.

After we prayed, the meeting ended and something seemed to break open. Hungry hands stretched out, eager to touch every one of ours, it seemed. The support group members roamed the room to eagerly clasp our hands in theirs, with deep bows and eye contact. They often leaned into the gentle Ethiopian shoulder-butt that signifies added affection.

That evening at our team debriefing, with only a few flashlights by which to see each other, it was difficult to talk of anything but our encounter with the support group. After everyone else had shared, I shined a light toward Jen in the shadows and asked if she had any thoughts. She quietly shared the rest—and the best—of the story.

As we had given our heartfelt handshakes and said our goodbyes to the group, Jen had staked out a strategic spot near the exit in order to hug the remaining women as they left. One by one they had acquiesced, until the last woman came up. Jen recalled, "At first she only wanted to shake my hand, though she'd seen me hug others. But I pulled her close. Her initial stiffness melted away and she hungrily hugged me back with her head on my shoulder. Then suddenly she arched up and I felt her lips softly kiss my neck." Leaping over every language barrier and every stigma, the kiss communicated everything.

After Jen's story, there was nothing left to say. We were all glad now to be in shadow, each lost in our own thoughts, our own prayers.

Everyone should have the opportunity to touch people living with HIV. Each person in our group had confronted their fears, their judgments, and their responses. Jen's response of unguarded compassion had melted a hungry heart. And when she shared her story, even more hungry hearts were melted.

A Global Day of Prayer

October 1 marks the start of World Vision's fiscal year. Around the globe, every office dedicates the entire day to prayer and thanksgiving. The World Vision U.S. and World Vision International offices on the West Coast of the United States are the last legs of a marathon that starts 16 hours earlier in Australia and moves around the world through almost 100 countries. It's a stunning and unique commitment in an organization of this size.

This year I attended the Global Day of Prayer with World Vision U.S., near Seattle. I look forward each year to concentrated prayer for global needs, but on this day we also spend a powerful time praying for donors. This year there must have been over 15,000 donor prayer requests—more than in any previous year. Each of the attendees (well over 500) was given 25 cards of handwritten prayer requests that donors had mailed in with their contributions. For an hour we prayed silently over each request and wrote postcard notes to the supplicants.

What a powerful reminder this was of why I love World Vision. This organization impacts 100 million people in need each year in nearly 100 countries. Yet how does that impact happen? Through the faithful widow's mite and through the hearts of the humble.

Today we intimately encountered the private petitions of those humble enough to ask for prayer, to pour their hearts out to some stranger. A stranger, yes, but not a faceless institution or bureaucracy. Rather, a partner in ministry. Whether from a sense of connection or out of desperation, they asked for prayer as an act of faith.

Breathe slowly as you read a few requests I had the privilege of lifting up:

- *That God gives us a bigger home, so we can take in more foster kids—to love those children.*
- *For my father to not be in pain.*
- *That God would forgive me from my sexual sins and that Jesus lets me up in heaven.*
- *Heal fractures in my family.*
- *My children and my grandchildren. My sponsored children's health and their families. All the poor and abandoned children.*
- *All the hungry and homeless people; my needs are minor compared to theirs.*
- *Friendship with other single seniors who love our Lord. Sometimes I feel lonely.*
- *For my 10-year-old, that if it is God's will He would spare her the ravages of this disease.*
- *That my friend leaving prison would heed the Spirit and avoid trouble.*
- *For a young mother with life-threatening cancer.*
- *For my husband's return to our girls and to me. He doesn't see them or even return their calls.*
- *I haven't worked in almost a year: Pray for work.*
- *For my granddaughter on drugs and on parole, and for her twins now being raised by her own middle-aged parents.*
- *That we could pay off our credit card debt so our family of six could adopt children in need.*

The final prayer card stopped me in my tracks: An 87-year-old woman was distraught because some ministry told her that God had led them to her and they really needed her money. She had given them all she could give, so now her sponsorship pledge would be late. She asked prayer for forgiveness from God in case she'd made wrong decisions on giving away her money. (I'm keeping that one in my office.)

Praying for these requests was such a privilege. I kept the cards and prayed through them again later. I was struck by the reality that a tapestry of donors large and small hangs in the banquet hall of the King. The tapestry includes people rich and poor, young and old, black and white, highly educated and illiterate, many with hearts far larger than their checking accounts. All of us woven together into a fabric diverse and beautiful; each thread a small yet infinitely precious part. One part prays for another. None is greater than the others.

No gift is too small or too large to fit in an offering plate lifted up to the Lord, mingled with the incense of the fervent prayers of the fragile and the hurting who gave what they could. Gave to meet another's need in the midst of their own needs. "I'm not working, but here's my gift and my prayer request." "I'm broken-hearted; here's my contribution to help heal the broken."

My heart hurts for these needs. This time, it's not the needs of the recipients but of the givers. For as we are all wounded healers, we are givers who are also in need of receiving.

After the prayer session, I sat alone writing this while everyone ate their box lunches in the foyer. Alone with my thoughts. Alone with my prayer cards. Spent. A friend walked over to chat and I couldn't do it. This was a holy hour; I was in a sanctuary. I had just walked through the private dreams and pains of 25 faithful partners in this ministry.

I'm in awe of the fellowship of saints that is the World Vision donor family, and of the privilege and the awesome responsibility of stewarding their sacred trust. Everything World Vision has comes from God, but it comes through the hands of His servants, many of whom—maybe all of whom—give to alleviate the suffering of others even in the midst of their own suffering.

Walls and WWJD

Walls. They can be a good thing, especially when they provide safety to those inside, like kids and pets. But I've been interacting a lot lately with walls that are designed to keep people out, not in.

I took a group to Tijuana last week. Over dinner the evening before we left, I spoke with one of them about her plans for her eighth trip to Palestine to visit World Vision projects among the poorest.

Ever notice that when you hear about a trip to Israel you think of one type of trip, and when you hear about a trip to Palestine it sounds completely different? In fact, it is different. A friend of mine who just came back from Israel admitted that his guide didn't take him to any Palestinian areas, not even to Bethlehem, because of security concerns. Yet the veteran visitor I spoke with is one of a small group of three women who can't wait to get back to Palestine, to be with and to pray with those who are excluded, ethnically and economically, from the prospering state on the other side of the foreboding, separating wall. She told me of her passion for this region and how these trips have changed both her perspective and her life as she, a well-to-do, white American suburbanite, has come to know the poor and powerless beyond that wall of separation.

The next morning we passed through a different wall—the U.S. border with Mexico. Once more I stood on a hilltop of dilapidated (though improving) squatters' homes in the Pedregal neighborhood of Tijuana and squinted through the haze at glittering downtown San Diego and fabled Coronado—cities that represent, for the residents of Pedregal, an unattainable Oz across a field not of wild poppies but of concrete, barbed wire, and police dogs.

But Pedregal has another wall now, also designed to keep out undesirables. You see, in perhaps the most puzzling and incongruous transformation I've personally witnessed, the Valley of Garbage, which we previously had to skirt via a rutted dirt road to get to Pedregal, has been replaced by tidy tract housing. What was once a huge eyesore is now a neighborhood of cracker-box homes with paved streets, curbs, drivable cars, and middle-class families.

What a change of scenery for these slum-dwelling friends of ours! Yet quite far beyond them economically. Most of World Vision's national staff in Tijuana tell me they could not afford these homes, which cost from $40,000 to $70,000. The Pedregal residents could afford them even less.

Still, the nice, new homes seem to be spurring visible improvements in the slum area too, from community-organized trash cleanups to the omnipresent stacks of cinder block, as Pedregal's residents invest in their own humble community and homes. That's good news!

We first encountered this trash-to-treasure metamorphosis one year ago when the first tract homes were being constructed. We drove down a new paved street, slicing through what had previously been a dirt field where my grandkids and the local kids had played soccer two years earlier. The street ended right at Pedregal, flanked by new homes.

How incredible, I thought, if somehow the middle- and lower-class neighbors could live this way, one neighborhood nuzzled right up to the next. But come on: Would the middle-class moms soon moving in really allow their kids such easy access to the slum, or the reverse? I hoped so, but I had my doubts.

Sadly, this year we had to drive around the new neighborhood instead of through it. A big wall now separates the two communities, shielding the richer neighbors from our dear friends, the poorer ones.

It's interesting what happens when one befriends first the power-less, the moneyless. One sees the world from the bottom of the pool looking up, not the reverse. And a wall we might normally perceive as providing prudent protection suddenly looks instead like a wall of exclusion. It's this bottom-dweller perspective that my Palestine-loving friends are discovering.

Of course, we left there only to cross back over our American wall of protection (or is it exclusion?) at the border.

As I drove home thinking of walls and those they exclude, I recalled a saying I'd read on a t-shirt while visiting famed Olvera Street in the original historic "village" of Los Angeles. The saying is a new twist on the great "WWJD" challenge, and one just as haunting. It speaks of our own attempts at walls and exclusion, a question worth contemplating, maybe from the bottom of the pool looking up:

Who Would Jesus Deport?

The Golden State

As a Midwestern transplant to California 20 years ago, I always despised the mantra "you are what you drive," the idea that my mode of transportation is actually an extension of my personhood, an expression of the real me.

How vain, I thought. How Hollywood. What a capitulation to the onslaught of advertising and the consumptive lifestyle.

Fast-forward to 2008. There I am getting something from the trunk of my clean, late-model Honda Accord with its heated seats, parked in my clean, late-model town with nary a blade of grass out of place. A woman drives by on the street outside our condo in a boxy, 12-year-old van with dirty, saucer-shaped hubcaps. I caught one quick glance and vomited up the thought: "Why would anyone drive something that looks like that? I mean, come on, where's her self-esteem?"

And there it was, just that quickly, lying on the sidewalk of my mind. I'd judged this woman as though she'd gone to an expensive restaurant dressed in her pajamas. "Why would anyone do that?"

Move me to the head of the class of conspicuous consumers. An honorary native of the Golden State.

What bugs me so much about my mental belch is that it betrays in me a growing disconnect with the reality of most of the world: the assumption that anyone can afford what I can afford and that only bad taste or poor decision-making keeps others from choosing better, having better, wanting better.

Because any self-respecting person surely would, right? Doesn't she realize that driving that uninspiring hunk of dirty metal in south Orange County is a direct reflection of her bad taste? Everybody knows that here, a clean, current-model car doesn't make you respectable. It simply makes you acceptable.

How shocking for someone in my line of work! I would never think like this while in Tijuana, or even near the World Vision offices in south-central L.A. But I was in my safe neighborhood cocoon, an unsanctified cloister, set apart from the world's reality and diversity. And when the tiniest hint of that world drove by, I sent up a knee-jerk snort of mental outrage.

Another unsightly glimpse into my world, the world of the "haves." Maybe the "must-haves." The world of the top 3 percent.

It's true: According to GlobalRichList.com, almost all Americans are in the top 3 percent of global family incomes. Most of us are well into the top 1 percent.

Over time I've gradually and mostly unintentionally insulated myself from the "other" 97 percent through where I live, what I drive, and now, by what I think when I'm not on my guard.

I don't know what to do in those situations other than repent, ask God's forgiveness, and ask Him to scrape off the insulation from my heart once again. I'm supposed to be transforming into the image of His Son, but at these times I feel I'm being transformed from someone who knew, and lived near, the poor (by American standards, of course) into a rich kid who looks out the bars of his school playground at the dirty-faced street urchins beyond and wonders uncomprehendingly what their life must be like. Yet who is also unspeakably glad to be safely on his own side of the bars.

So I repent. I reject the impervious judge I've become and I do everything except seriously change the lifestyle that led me there. There's a deepening sadness in me, a sadness of dis-incarnation, of moving inexorably away from what Jesus moved toward. And whom he moved toward. One "harmless" life choice at a time, slipping ever deeper into the insulating and isolating quicksand.

As a last resort, at least I can still recognize it, name it, and disclaim it, calling out to God that I too might be saved. "Well then," the disciples asked Jesus nervously, "if the rich can't be saved, who can be?"

"With man this is impossible," the Teacher assured them. Then He quickly added, "But with God all things are possible" (Matthew 19:25-26).

Thanks be to God.

Pizza and Proximity

Bart is a World Vision donor and personal friend who lives in an exclusive beachside community. He told me a beautiful story this week about how his wife, Debi, had sought out the needy beyond their invisible gates.

Debi had brought pizza to a Christian outreach lunch for high school athletes at the private school their sons attend. The school is near them, but in a semi-notorious, mixed-bag community. Every area has its "other side of the tracks" that's generally avoided; in Bart and Debi's area, this is it.

Debi had bought extra pizza to make sure there was enough for all who might show up, since this was the first time she'd provided the food. When the event was over, she still had seven pizzas left.

On her own, Debi decided to drive to a nearby park where she had heard some homeless people were staying. She approached a mother and boy in the park and offered them one of her pizzas. The boy turned to his mother: "See, Mom? I told you we would be all right."

What a story must be behind his comment! The boy comforted his worried mother, who feared for their well-being. Perhaps they were new to the park, to homelessness? Perhaps this mother was at the end of her resources, her rope, her hope? But her son still held out hope, still maintained his boyish buoyancy. Maybe she wanted to believe him, to believe like him, to have faith: faith that maybe God knows the plans He has for even them, and that they are plans for good, plans for a future and a hope.

The boy's words suggest they'd just recently had such a discussion, where the youngster tried to play the role of confident comforter for his worried mother. Oh, to be like a child again.

And faith comes through for them! Faith which is "the confidence that what we hope for will actually happen; it gives us assurance about things we cannot see" (Hebrews 11:1, NLT).

You think I'm taking a sweet story and trying to overanalyze and over-glamorize it? Maybe, but here's what happened next.

Debi was so blessed by the boy's comment that she offered them a second pizza. I don't know what comes to your mind, but when my friend Bart paused at that point in the story, I anticipated that the two had ravenously and gratefully eaten both pizzas, or sold one to make some needed money. Terrific! And if they couldn't eat or sell it all, oh well—it would have gone to waste anyway.

I honestly thought that, because I don't live among the poor. But this mother and son did. They graciously declined the second pizza and pointed Debi to the homeless people on the other side of the park who likely were hungry too.

Beautiful. Like the manna God provided, which couldn't be hoarded and wouldn't last overnight. When you don't have a refrigerator, the practicality of that Bible story becomes clear. She who had been offered much did not take too much, so that he who had little did not have too little. Sure, it was just a lukewarm, leftover pizza, but this decision had more impact on them than a $100 decision does for most of us.

Beyond that, this homeless twosome was certainly more aware of the needs of others because of their close proximity to them. This story is a tangible illustration of how being near people in need makes us more sensitive and can change the choices we make. The choice they made.

I was also struck by Debi's choices that day. Anyone could think of plenty of uses for leftover pizza with family and neighbors. But somehow Debi remembered hearing about this park. She had the guts to say "yes" to the prompting she felt. She searched for the park, got out of her car, walked up to homeless people, and passed out food—by herself.

Where she lives, this is not a daily occurrence, to be sure.

Yet Debi broke through the barriers of distance, unfamiliarity, and fear to have a close, personal encounter with some fellow human beings who could use what she had. An encounter close enough to hear a boy's intimate words of comfort directed to his distressed mother, words Debi will never forget. And she encountered firsthand the rich perspective of one who lives among the poor, the have-enough mentality of a so-called "have-not."

Somehow, I don't think this outing at the park will be Debi's last.

Attempting Beauty

Last month, our church class watched a video of Bishop Desmond Tutu. He was telling an American congregation about the post-apartheid era in South Africa, specifically about the Truth and Reconciliation Commission (TRC) there. The TRC spent 10 years attempting to find a third way to deal with the horrible crimes committed by both sides during apartheid, something between punitive retribution and national amnesia.

Bishop Tutu told moving stories of forgiveness, of perpetrators coming forward and admitting guilt in exchange for pardons, yes, but even more—of perpetrators weeping with their victims or the victims' families, and of a traveling court that touched many parts of that deeply wounded nation with healing.

I knew enough of the Commission's work to know that it garnered mixed reviews along the way. It was neither a total success nor a complete failure. Yet here was Bishop Tutu touting its most poignant achievements with powerful stories of reconciliation. Still, I wondered a bit if we'd get the full scoop.

Then he admitted that not everyone was ready or willing to accept reconciliation—Steve Biko's family, for instance. Biko, who was arguably a more energetic and magnetic black leader back in 1977 than the imprisoned Nelson Mandela, notoriously died in jail during apartheid as a result of repeated beatings by his white jailers. His family wanted justice finally served after this heinous, state-authorized crime.

Bishop Tutu talked of how difficult and costly reconciliation really is, "so costly that it cost God His Son on the cross."

Honestly, I've often felt a bit uncomfortable with that phrase; it sometimes strikes me as emotional over-reaching, at its worst something used by gospel pitchmen coming in for the big close.

But at that moment I was still thinking of the Biko family, whose story I knew to be at the level of a Kennedy or King assassination-of-hope for many black South Africans at that time. Not to mention the fact that the crime was committed by their own government.

I thought of the Biko family's reality and of their inability to reconcile, by the legally binding terms of the TRC at least, and I felt their pain: the pain of what might have been; of the demeaning nature of the nationwide, institutionalized white supremacy that had scorched their family like the sun through a magnifying glass; and of the tremendous pressure now to reconcile so the TRC could put another feather in its cap.

But the family knew the pain full well. They knew what it would cost to forgive what they could not forget. They were the ones sinned against.

In empathizing with them, I realized how costly reconciliation truly is, how much more pain it would cost them to lay all that down. More costly than Bishop Tutu's words alone could express.

The story opened my heart, and Bishop Tutu poured in a truth that I usually have trouble digesting: all of this family's feelings, a million times over, couldn't express how sinned-against was the God who stooped down, uninvited, and gave His Son to those who would hate, mock, abuse, and kill Him. To reconcile with us. "Costly" doesn't begin to express it.

The Biko family had every reason not to reconcile when the cost was forgiving a past, unpunished transgression. God, who by all rights should have held his nose and simply said, "to hell with the lot of you," instead voluntarily walked right toward the transgression that hadn't even happened yet, fully knowing that it would. All for people who didn't ask for reconciliation or even give a rip about it.

This became fresh and heroic reconciliation to me. For me. And the good bishop wasn't trying to convince anyone, anyway. No clever hook. Just a man who gets it, because he walks with so many Bikos and others who have been sinned against, and he knows the depth of their pain.

After the video, someone in class asked if the TRC had really worked. Is there less crime now in majority-led South Africa as a result? Were race relations better? I knew the answer was unclear. Ask any South African transplant to America about the crime rate there today. I was in South Africa at the height of apartheid's police state, and again a couple of years ago, when I drove past foreboding residential walls topped with razor wire and glass shards.

But even while Bishop Tutu was still speaking, I got it. This wasn't about him pretending that his country's monumental attempt at national reconciliation had been a complete success. The evil of apartheid went too deep, too long, too hard, and too many people were involved. There were too many feelings, too many gaping wounds.

But this dear minister of the gospel was standing up and unapologetically declaring signs: signs of the kingdom of God, a kingdom of reconciliation, where mercy one day triumphs completely over judgment. He wasn't reporting; he was painting. He was declaring beauty in the midst of ugliness.

The other day I read the line: "Lord, please bless those who attempt beauty rather than curse ugliness."

Amen. What more can any of us do than attempt beauty? And then celebrate that beauty together, whenever and wherever we find it. Proclaim it from the rooftops and declare each patch holy ground on which to plant the flag of God's kingdom reign.

May His kingdom come on earth, in its fullness, soon. And may we in the meantime attempt beauty rather than curse ugliness.

After all, isn't that what the cross is all about?

Lifeboats

I've been thinking lately about lifeboat ethics in a flagging economy, lamenting those decisions we make in hunker-down times that can effectively reduce our circle of concern. But recently, I encountered some encouraging signposts.

The annual luncheon for the Orange County chapter of Women of Vision, a dedicated group that raises funds for World Vision programs around the world, was held last month. The speaker was Patricia Heaton of "Everybody Loves Raymond" fame and co-producer of the film "Amazing Grace," about William Wilberforce and the fight to end slavery in Britain.

Patricia gave a lovely talk. But what struck me most was the integration of her life and activities. Her film and acting ventures are designed to make money while making a values statement; her businesses provide training and jobs for inner-city women; her church giving underwrites the buses that bring in kids from Watts and Compton. A kingdom intentionality in each endeavor, coupled with a heart for those who are on the outside looking in. She said, "It's so important to us to do work that we are proud of, work that has some meaning and humanity."

The thing I'll probably remember longest was a story related to her family's underwriting of an orphanage outside Tijuana, which they've done for some years. When the TV writers went on strike in 2007, Patricia e-mailed the orphanage director asking for prayer and preparing him for the possibility that they would no longer be able to provide the same level of support if her income were to decline.

A few hours later, she wrote him back: "Ignore my last e-mail. We're with you regardless."

In those few hours, she had reprioritized what goes into her lifeboat, if and when she needs to prepare one. I have absolutely no idea what method she used to make her decision, as we didn't have a chance to talk about it afterward, but I'd love to think it went something like this: If we have to choose, will we keep our four boys in private school and take the vacation our family has been planning for, or support 50 parentless children in Mexico? When is my provision for my family related to their necessities, and when is it optional?

Granted, Patricia and her husband had committed years ago to underwrite the orphanage's entire operating budget, so they'd taken on a unique mantle of financial responsibility. But they'd done so voluntarily, which already says a great deal about their priorities.

It was a rather radical step, and one that most of us couldn't make at that level—though in fact we do make a similar choice whenever we send a disadvantaged student to camp, sponsor a child, or make an ongoing pledge to a special church project, forcing us to make the same calculations during financial tough times.

Patricia started with the typical knee-jerk lifeboat response: "Well, my situation has changed and I won't be able to continue my support." But she reprioritized and instead said, "Well, my situation has changed. Our family will have to make some choices!"

As I was hanging around after most attendees had left, a colleague who was also at the luncheon told me that she has recently been contacting elderly donors who have put World Vision into their estate plans, to thank them and hear their stories. She talked to a woman who lives on only her Social Security check, yet still sponsors six children every month. This elderly lady said, "Paula, I only have 82 cents to get me through the rest of this month, but God will provide; He always has." Paula related two or three equally touching stories of faithfulness and trust in God. As she talked, she began to cry.

My head and heart were too full to connect the dots then, but I realize now that she was talking of the same principle that confronted Patricia, brought down to a widow's-mite, bite-size scale that speaks to my life. We all have lifeboat times. But somewhere out there, sailing in the same rough waters, are saints of God, poor and rich and everything in between, who are taking the tack less chosen, throwing out some of their own stuff so more people can get into the boat with them.

Hebrews 12:1 spurs us to "throw off everything that hinders and the sin that so easily entangles, and let us run with perseverance the race marked out for us." The apostle Paul, whom many Bible scholars believe to be the author of Hebrews, was shipwrecked off the coast of Malta (I've gone swimming in the bay where the ship's passengers all safely swam ashore). Every one of those passengers made it because they'd thrown all the ship's cargo overboard to get close enough to land to survive the waters. If Hebrews had been written in light of this harrowing experience, the author might have chosen a nautical analogy: "So throw overboard everything that hinders and entangles, and sail with steadfast perseverance the course marked out for us."

After all, lifeboats are for saving the people, not the baggage.

Making All Things New

I slumped onto the pew kneeler at one of my favorite sanctuaries, Serra Chapel at Mission San Juan Capistrano—the oldest operating church building in California, known as the "jewel" of the historic Spanish missions that dot the coast. My heart was heavy from family issues, disappointment that I'd contracted the swine flu and had to cancel a trip to Palestine, and gnawing memories from a recent project visit to Tijuana. I gazed above me at the giant, dark painting of Christ on the cross, Mary at His side, the figurative sword of the Scriptures depicted by the artist as literally piercing her heart as she too gazes at Him, her dreams shattered.

My mind jumped to the scene in the movie "The Passion of the Christ" where an exhausted Jesus, pinned yet again under the heavy cross on the Via Dolorosa, turns to His mother and, with utter pathos, through blood-stained teeth, exclaims, "Look, Mother. I make all things new!"

I pondered the venerable painting before me: What is it about this Jesus hanging on a cross, completely humiliated and defeated, that evokes any sense of victory or hope? Why does this act of total capitulation still stir me?

My mind turned finally to my own reason for being there: to seek, through some spiritual work, an understanding of the angst inside me after my Tijuana experience. Why was it so haunting to me, so paralyzing? Objectively speaking, I would have to consider it a fabulous trip, one of my best ever to see World Vision's work among the poorest communities there. We met hardworking, inspiring people who were fighting their way to a better life despite the odds stacked against them. Frankly, I should have been delighted. And in the past,

I would have been.

But the morning after the visit (a Saturday), as I leisurely laid in bed, I remembered dear Lourdes. Lourdes is about my age; she's a single grandmother who owns a convenience store in a shabby squatter area. Lourdes has diabetes, though thanks to her business, she is able to pay for her treatments and monthly checkups. I first met her a year ago, and today Lourdes looks decidedly better than she did then. Though her eyes still look tired, her smile is infectious.

Not only had she made these gains, but in the intervening year Lourdes had also built a sturdy new house of cinder block right on top of her store. Last year we'd walked through her previous home, which was constructed of recycled American garage doors. Large, inexpensive but treasured paintings of Jesus and Mary hung from the crossbeams. Her new house sits like a beacon, a visible declaration of the progress her business is bringing, not only to her extended family, but to herself.

Lourdes herself is a beacon of inspiration. Despite her diabetes, she works seven days a week. So do her daughters, who sell her tamales to the workers in the *maquiladoras* (foreign-owned export assembly plants), which also operate every day of the week.

As Lourdes and I talked, I was reminded of a widow of similar age and demeanor whom I'd met a few years ago in Mexico City. That woman owned a storefront hardware shop in a hillside slum. Thanks to her hard work and a precious microloan, she had tripled the size of her shop. She proudly announced that now she works only six and a half days a week; she is doing well enough that she can close on Sunday mornings and go to church. She used to be too embarrassed to go to church anyway, because she didn't have anything to put into the offering plate. Now she does. Recalling the woman's story and Lourdes' portraits of Jesus in her home last year, I told Lourdes that I hoped in another year she would be able to slow down to six workdays a week and be able to go to church, as well.

As I lingered in my bed that Saturday, I remembered my fellow grandparent Lourdes and her grind-it-out reality. I knew that I'd catch up on e-mail and do some related work that day. But I'd do it when I felt like it—if I felt like it. I knew I had two days ahead of me that were pretty much my own. I have time to go to church on Sundays.

Living comfortably a mere 90 miles from Lourdes' house, I have health insurance. When I'm sick, the doctors and medicines are covered but for my modest co-pay. And I have sick days available, so that I still get paid even when I'm ill.

All the realities of the unequal opportunities life has presented to me and to my cross-border neighbor Lourdes cascaded into my mind. They drowned out the usual feelings of joy and inspiration that I would have experienced at what she has managed to accomplish in life despite those inequalities. Worse yet, I began to wonder secretly if what I do for people like her through World Vision is merely like wallpapering a moldy wall: The room looks fresh and cheerful, but the underlying structures are scandalously unsound.

So today, I decided to go through a spiritual exercise to find the invitation hidden inside my uncomfortable feelings. As I allowed the feelings to come and didn't deny them, I sensed not only disappointment but also shame—shame for being part of our world's unequal opportunities and personally benefiting from that inequality. And shame if I've been detached and disaffected, like the gentlemen solicitors in Charles Dickens' *A Christmas Carol* who try to pry an insignificant donation from old Ebenezer Scrooge, all dressed in their proper finery. "At this festive season of the year, Mr. Scrooge, it is more than usually desirable that we should make some slight provision for the poor and destitute ..." Privilege speaking thus to privilege about the under-privileged does not seem in keeping with Jesus' example of identification with the poor.

Am I but a Dickens caricature?

Yet, moving now to the mission garden, surrounded by its centuries-old beauty and the warmth of the afternoon sun, I felt the comfort of the Lord telling me: "I am the God who sees everything, forgiving much and correcting but a little. Why do you fear that I stand over you to correct you? I said a cup of cold water in my name will not go unrewarded. Don't you believe me? You fear you will look over your shoulder and see me scowling, shaking a finger. Yet you will see me full of compassion, slow to anger. I know how limited is your mind, your view, your understanding. You don't see a fraction of what I see in your actions and inactions—and their impact. But I am the God who looks for good, for obedience, who will not break a bruised reed. This is the God you will see. Turn around! See Me! Feel My warm touch on your shoulder, My beauty caressing you through the sun and flowers and birds and water around you."

Somehow, this was the breakthrough word I needed, a sense that God is inviting me to look deeper, but not in order to find fault. Instead, He gave me a renewed paradigm, one that gains energy from those who beat the odds and becomes motivated to do more to change the uneven playing field as a result, rather than be paralyzed by it. New eyes that can see everything and say, "Lourdes, you inspire me! You make me want to work harder for a more just world. Why? Because you are not waiting for life to be fair. You are working as hard as you can. You are not complaining; you don't have the time. But your hard work for your family makes me want to pitch in with you and help you throw off the yoke of inequality and injustice. To create a world where your grandchildren have the same advantages as my grandchildren. Where you have the same access to healthcare and insurance that I have. Where you can have vacation days like I have. Don't stop! Progress is slow and uneven, but it happens. My grandfather had a life not unlike yours.

May your grandchildren have a life not unlike mine. And, one day, the lion will lie down with the lamb. The hummingbirds will land in your garden too, a place of beauty, a place of peace and joy."

I see it as I sit here in the old mission grounds: New beauty sprouts and blooms even from the ruins. Make that my work, Lord, as it is Your work.

"Let us then approach the throne of grace with confidence, so that we may receive mercy and find grace to help us in our time of need" (Hebrews 4:16). This is the invitation and the grace I've received today: an invitation to see and to bless signs of a coming kingdom, an invitation to hope, to again embrace optimism at progress, to have eyes of faith in a God who is making all things new.

Wasta

Wasta. It's my favorite Arabic word, and I saw it in action this morning around 7 a.m.

Wasta means something like power, and connections, and the ability to make things happen. I learned the word while visiting my daughter Karey when she lived in Jordan with the Peace Corps 10 years ago, and it has stayed with me ever since. It's amazing how often it's the perfect word in a situation, though there is no exact English equivalent.

This morning I was reminded of how much *wasta* my wife has, as we heard the garbage truck rumbling into the school parking lot across the street. A couple weeks ago, we were awakened several mornings before 6 a.m. by the sound of that same truck. (Okay, let me admit right here that neither of us is an early bird, and the only worms we ever catch are nightcrawlers.)

Anyway, though we are nobody special and live in a relatively small, generic condo, Janet phoned City Hall and learned that in fact there is an ordinance that prohibits trucks like this from beginning their work until 7 a.m.

That evening, Janet told me that she'd left a voice message for the appropriate official, and that soon he had called her back and gotten the details. He told her of the ordinance, and then he hung up and promptly called the garbage company. The garbage company claimed they were already following this ordinance and asked some questions; the official called Janet back, found out the answers, and called the garbage company a second time, and then he called Janet yet again to assure her the problem had been taken care of.

Unfortunately, the next day the problem happened again. So Janet called back and told the official, who apparently read the riot act to the garbage company. Ever since then, the truck has rumbled into the school right at 7 a.m.

For many of us, there is nothing at all remarkable about this story; it's simply an example of city government working as it's supposed to work, and sometimes does work, if perhaps more often in smaller towns like ours. But to other readers, this story would be extraordinary because their gender or ethnicity or economic status is such that they would be categorically excluded from this kind of access to the powers that be. But in our town that day, taxpayer Janet had the *wasta* and the problem was fixed.

The wandering livestock herders of the Afar desert in Ethiopia often refer to themselves as "the forgotten people." I think many times our visiting travelers there don't recognize the significance of that self-definition. To be forgotten means to be ignored. To be ignored means to be denied the services that others receive, that one should receive. To be forgotten, as the Afar define themselves, starts not with their status as world citizens but as citizens of their very own country, and then goes deeper to impact even their psyche and self-worth.

This is a huge aspect of the social sustainability that World Vision works to foster in marginalized communities. The social margin is a lonely and powerless place to be.

I remember one visit to our Tijuana project a couple of years ago during which we met many of the women leaders of the project. As we were getting ready to leave, the group of visitors asked, "Where are all the men?" Just then, almost as if on cue, a beat-up old station wagon rumbled across the dirt road. I'm ashamed to admit, if a station wagon like that rumbled down our street full of four Mexican men, our first thought might be to lock our doors. Four men did emerge from the vehicle, including Mr. Roberto. Mr. Roberto, whom I'd met before, is something of an elder statesman in his community.

Through our translator, we learned that these four men had just been to City Hall to negotiate terms for becoming owners of the land on which their homes stood. I marveled at this and asked why World Vision staff had not gone to the meeting with them. I was aware of how marginalized the residents were in these squatter settlements.

I learned that in the past, the staff had accompanied them and had even set up the meetings and served as an honest broker. But now the community's own members (well, the men anyway, but that's a start) were sufficiently empowered and confident in their abilities to negotiate with City Hall. They'd gone all alone, as their community's official representatives. There they learned of requirements to improve ground percolation and other safety issues that would need to be addressed before the city would be willing to grant them status as an official community, leading to sewer lines, proper sanitation, and the ability to acquire their homesteaded land. As they address those issues and move the process forward, these community residents will lead the charge, with World Vision's local staff coaching from the sidelines.

Empowerment.

The number of issues that cascade off of land ownership is huge, including one's willingness to actually improve his or her unsafe, ramshackle home, one's commitment to the cleanliness of the community, and most deeply, one's sense of personal and community pride.

These are issues that go so far beyond the impact of providing a school or constructing a community center or the provision of clean water. This is why these strategies are called social sustainability—they build up the community's self-definition, their belief in their ability to effect change, to make a better life for their children, to have a sustained voice. It means "We matter."

Wasta-making. Imagine a world where what Scripture says of our inherent value is actually played out in the halls of power, for everyone.

"Thy kingdom come on earth ..."

One final addendum to Janet's own success story. The garbage truck came at 6:50 a.m. today, and Janet noticed. I'm afraid she may be limbering up to flex her *wasta* again. But since today was the last day of school, and therefore of garbage pickup, I think City Hall is safe for a couple of months. In September, I may run for cover.

Bump on the Road

A couple Saturdays ago I was lamenting my current lack of local, hands-on ministry involvement. So when a musician friend e-mailed a couple hours later to ask if Janet and I would help him lead worship at a street-side memorial service for a homeless man in Santa Ana the following morning, it was hard to take seriously my usual excuses why the idea is nice but the timing is bad, blah, blah. I'm so glad I fought off the excuses and said yes. Because I experienced not only a window into the reality of the street but into the heart of the late Jeff Bump.

My musician friend had received conflicting information about the gathering, and wasn't sure whether it was a memorial or a normal outreach service put together by people from his suburban church. And when we arrived, there seemed to be as many volunteers ready to serve the free breakfast as there were partakers. This kind of drive-in programming, seemingly not tied to any ongoing local ministry, never excites me much.

Because of the conflicting information on the focus of the gathering, my friend decided to choose safe, contemporary worship songs from the suburban white church, many of which are lovely but unfamiliar to those attending.

I admit I didn't have a very good attitude when we arrived half an hour in advance to quickly rehearse the songs—or so we thought. Turns out we had the wrong start time and they needed us to begin immediately! So we rushed to set up and jumped right in with barely a "Hail Mary" prayer for God's Spirit. The small, U-shaped asphalt patch where we met, created by the windowless walls of three unfriendly buildings, opened onto a noisy street that competed all-too-effectively with our humble sound system.

We seemed more like a distraction than anything; most people simply stared or kept eating their breakfast. I felt about as relevant as a singing duck—a curiosity to be watched, not joined. Mercifully, the singing time ended and we could sit down. Personally, I was deflated and regretted that my excuses hadn't won the argument the day before.

Then a street-savvy preacher got up and put his open Bible on the pulpit: an old pizza box duct-taped to a folding stand. He stood next to a Dumpster protected by a chainlink fence and welcomed everyone. After he read from his Bible and spoke for just a few minutes about his deceased friend Jeff Bump, he invited those who knew Jeff to come and speak.

That's when we had church.

One after another they came up to pay respects to a fellow resident of the streets. Jeff's photo and a small American flag were taped to the bare wall behind us, the latter to acknowledge that Jeff was a Vietnam veteran. He was only a couple years older than me, though with his full, white, flowing beard and kind but weary grey eyes, he could easily have passed for my father's contemporary.

A young woman stood to tell how Jeff would share anything he had. How Jeff would see her taking drugs with her boyfriend and encourage them to stop. But, she said after seriously losing her composure, he always added, "Even if you keep doing the drugs, I will always be your friend." My heart latched onto her and I wondered: Would an ounce of that unconditional love from someone years earlier have changed her life's trajectory?

An older man who was missing one arm said, "Jeff was no saint, but he was a good partner. On the streets, you gotta have a partner. He shared everything. He'd give you his last dime. I'd see him in the mornings having his favorite wake-up drink—vodka—and he even shared his wake-up. If you never been on the streets, you got no idea how generous that is. He was no saint, but he was generous; he even shared his wake-up."

A toothless woman told us with tears that "Amazing Grace" was Jeff's favorite song. She brought her oversized boom box so she could play us the worst instrumental recording of the song I'd ever heard. While it played on, she waved her raised hands, without shame, in praise to the Lord who generously bestows grace on His children, not only to the broken but also to the cynical; praised be His name.

Then a guy introduced himself as Jeff's best friend. He was the first "cleaned-up" speaker we'd seen. He told us he'd lived with Jeff for two years on the streets, but Jeff was always telling him to quit drinking, even while Jeff continued to drink. "Jeff always believed in me and in my future," he said. Then he announced, "Well, I decided to believe Jeff. I've been sober seven months now, and I'm gonna keep going to honor Jeff!"

He talked on about the hope Jeff had, how he brought out the best in others, how they would bed down together behind houses and drink and then talk about the Bible together for hours. How Jeff staked out a street location near a pay phone where he would see a steady stream of prostitutes and drug dealers. And he'd urge them, "Don't do it!" probably at serious risk to himself. Maybe Kris Kristofferson knew someone like Jeff Bump when he wrote the profound truth in "Me and Bobby McGee": "Freedom's just another word for nothing left to lose." When there's nothing you're afraid to lose, you are thrillingly unshackled to do good. Jeff often used what little money and influence he had to make friends, to help others who needed it more than he did. Freedom.

Jeff's best friend wasn't done. He told us how their talks had transformed him, how Jeff had countered his friend's spiritual procrastination with his own gritty faith, holding onto Jesus with his dirty fingernails dug in. That he hopes he makes it into heaven, and he hopes to see Jeff there. I guess after you've experienced the vulnerability of the streets, it's easy to remember that even your eternal destiny is ultimately in God's hands alone, not some Reformation theologian's.

"Maybe you've been giving excuses and procrastinating too," he continued in his humble storytelling style. "Well, Jeff would say 'Don't wait!' He wouldn't want you to wait." This speaker's invitation to the Jesus road, an invitation to those who were already in the roads and on the streets, was one of most authentic evangelistic testimonies I've ever heard. Here was brokenness speaking to brokenness, a beggar telling other beggars where he'd found bread. No one issuing guaranteed tickets through the pearly gates, just a humble invitation to walk a new road that, God willing, might take you there.

When the sharing was over, our music team had enough sense to get up and lead everyone in "Amazing Grace." Grace seemed even more amazing that day.

But lovely as those lyrics are, we might have sung words even more confessional, more street-wise, more reflective of Jeff, from another Kris Kristofferson gem, "Why Me Lord":

If you think there's a way I can try to repay all I've taken from You
Maybe Lord I can show someone else what I've been through myself
on my way back to You
Lord help me Jesus I've wasted it so; Help me Jesus, I know what
I am.
Now that I know that I needed you so; Help me Jesus, my soul's
in your hands

The next evening, at a church harvest party, I sang that song . . . and I dedicated it to Jeff Bump.

In Good Company

Last Wednesday I had surgery to remove a cyst on one of my vocal cords. Surgery went well, but afterward I discovered my tongue wasn't working properly. The doctor believes I have a stunned nerve. No one knows how long it will last. He says my body will simply fix itself when (if?) it's good and ready. In the meantime, there's nothing to be done about it.

I was really frustrated at what a chore it was (and still is) to chew, swallow, and speak. Funny how a thing like that can affect my whole attitude—my peace, patience, and self-control. All the fruits of the Spirit go rotten overnight. I'm such a baby! Could this be the worst malady I've ever had to deal with? It's no fun, for sure. I bite my tongue daily, and when I talk my words are slurred, so I have to be very deliberate in my speech. As I labor to articulate, I self-consciously wonder if people think I'm mentally "slow."

The day after surgery I needed to work off some agitation and energy with a good, hard swim. As I started my laps in the pool, I discovered that it's also quite difficult now to sweep water from my mouth, especially during a flip turn. But as I stayed the course and concentrated, I choked less and less on the water and was able to have an almost-normal swim.

Even though it added fodder to the frustration I was trying to burn off, it was good to swim. But on this summer Saturday the city pool was quite full, and I had to share the only lap lane with a young woman. She had a toned physique and wore a one-piece swimmer's suit, but she was surprisingly slow. When I'd pass her, as I was learning to harness my errant tongue and keep from choking, I noticed that her breaststroke was possibly the worst I'd ever seen. There were no propulsive sweeping arms and frog-kicks, but rather a goofy curling up, almost into a face-down fetal position, then stretching out. She was really lousy, though she had an athlete's body. "Maybe she's a runner or aspiring triathlete who doesn't know the first thing about swimming," I thought.

Yet she kept swimming next to me for a good half-hour. I took off my training gloves near the end of my swim. She was standing at the pool wall also. I turned to communicate, but I wasn't supposed to be talking yet and was dealing with this tongue issue. So instead I lifted one hand, spread out all my fingers, quietly mouthed, "Fah moe!"and pointed down the lap lane to signal my final five laps. As I swam, I thought about whether I could find a nonverbal way to give her one or two tips on swimming when I was done, but when I stopped she'd already crossed under the lane line and was on the other side of the pool.

As I stood in the pool packing my gear, a woman in a lounge chair smiled lingeringly at me. At first I was flattered: I'd fought my way through a tough post-surgery swim and I was feeling good about it; maybe I was looking good, too! Then I wondered if maybe she'd heard my neighborly but pathetic attempt to speak to my lane partner.

Just then, a bouncy female voice said, "Thanks for swimming with me!" and my wannabe swim partner walked past, a big smile on her face, ambling on her toes with her arms flailing limp below the elbows and knees akimbo, teetering toward the restroom.

After a quick elbow-jab to myself ("You idiot!"), another set of lights in my head went on: I was being branded. Both the swimmer and the spectator saw me as disabled, too. The lounge chair smile had a friendly yet condescending, pat-on-the-head quality to it. I've employed that smile many times. Frankly, it felt demeaning to be smiled at from above like that, to be on the other side of that transaction for a change and remember my feelings from her side of it. She wasn't purposely looking down on me, but I wasn't her equal, either.

My swimmer friend, on the other hand, seemed to genuinely appreciate me, a fellow-struggler, doing our best together, getting good physical activity and not judging one another. Okay, I'd judged her a bit, but I'd like to think it was only as a coach judges a student. We formed a fellowship of uphill strugglers. She heard my stammering and awarded me immediate membership in a society I didn't ever want to be in—but was also somehow proud to be in.

She and I saw each other again as we walked out of the gates. I was tempted to strike up a conversation but quickly remembered I couldn't talk. And I thought better of it anyway. I sensed God was showing me something here that He didn't want me to miss, a firsthand experience with condescension. He also wanted to show me this alternate universe where less-than-"perfect" people draw strength from one another.

The timing of the experience was exquisite. God wasn't frustrated by my tongue problem nor panicked by it. I thought: Maybe this is the next chapter in my story, like it or not. The Author decides that, not me. In that moment, something in my attitude began to shift. My anxiety dissipated. I no longer felt like I was in an out-of-control crisis but setting out on a journey, a path downward from my rim-of–the-world highway of privilege, power, and position. A path of unknowing, of frustration, of humility, and of humiliation. A path that will require trust, and maybe some courage, to turn the page.

O, For a Brand-New Tongue to Sing

It was our second day in northern Tanzania. We rumbled down the rural road and pulled off next to a small building in a nondescript outcropping of civilization. Outside stood a dozen Maasai women waiting for our meeting to start and for the others to arrive. They seemed energetic and confident, so I engaged them in an informal video interview. Our translator worked busily beside me.

In the meantime, another 20 or so local people showed up, so we all moved into the building and onto low benches. At first I sat with the ladies, instead of on the front row across the aisle where the guests were supposed to sit. But it soon became clear that this was problematic for our translator, so I moved over. Some formalities have utility, as well.

This was an interesting group; they comprised the community care coalition (CCC) for this district. World Vision organizes these groups of local volunteers (mostly community members plus some religious and government leaders) who band together to respond to the destructive effects of HIV and AIDS in their midst. They care for orphans and vulnerable children living near them and with them, and they care for people living—and dying—with the virus. AIDS has shredded the renowned African social fabric in many places; the CCCs are the front line of personal care and the proving ground for new community coping mechanisms.

World Vision's long-term goal (and the focus for our trip) is to equip these CCCs to ultimately stand on their own and act as full-fledged local nonprofits, capable of running programs, managing budgets, receiving grants, and extending the reach of NGOs and government agencies into remote hamlets.

After meeting with this group, we saw evidence of those very outcomes when we visited a family of four sisters, aged 10 to 16, who fend for themselves. They were too ashamed to admit they were orphans, but both their parents had died four years ago and they'd lived alone ever since. Well, almost alone. A faithful CCC volunteer named Evelyn looks after them. The girls told us, "We love it when Evelyn comes. She is the only person who visits us."

Each home-visit volunteer in the CCC looks after 10 so-called child-headed households (a terrible term in that it reduces an unspeakable human tragedy to sociological jargon). The volunteers check in weekly. They make sure the children have food, encourage them to stay in school, pray with them, and distribute help that comes through the CCC (such as 10 chickens and a coop). They serve as extended families—as aunties—to children who have none.

Make no mistake: The volunteers are mostly moms, indignant women who think it's shameful that anyone's kids would be forced to live like this. Like so many women around the world, they are eager to find some way to turn their indignation into action.

On the way to this home, we stopped at a surprisingly large farmhouse (relatively speaking, of course). As it turns out, Evelyn had advocated on behalf of a mentally challenged girl from a different child-headed household after the girl had broken her leg. The girl simply didn't understand that she shouldn't move her leg, and she needed someone to watch over her for six weeks so her siblings could continue to work the fields and go to school. So Evelyn went to the farmer's wife and, woman-to-woman, showed her a tangible way she could help this child by letting her live with them. For six weeks. Simple, cost-free, yet immensely helpful.

Here's something you can do
A plow to put your hand to
It's not forever nor too much
But you can be God's loving touch

The lady said yes; the child was resting peacefully—at least until our entourage of *mzungu* (white people) lumbered into the dimly lit room and petrified her.

Let's go back to earlier in the day, when we were just getting to know these soldiers of passion and healing. As we each introduced ourselves, one volunteer started by saying *"Bwana asifewe!"* Our translator explained that the group isn't limited to Christians, but most members are believers, and a common greeting among believers is "Praise the Lord." In Swahili, *"Bwana asifewe."*

Asifewe. I scanned my mind's hard drive: "I know that word." Yes! It's in a Swahili worship song I'd often taught to American churches or other groups years ago as I led worship. I hadn't sung it in maybe five years, but as the introductions continued around the room, the tune and words came back in a flood. *"Yesu u hai leo, asifewe!"* ("Jesus is alive today, oh praise His name!")

Because I'd moved to the other bench, I was the very last person on the very last row to introduce myself. I did so and then said, "I think I know a Swahili worship song." "Oh, many of us know it," the translator exclaimed, "and you must sing it for us!" "No, no, but please, you sing it and I'll listen." "No, Cory, you must sing it—and we will join in."

Of course I sang it. Actually, we all sang it, arms swinging over our heads, round and round. I even added the descant on the (literally) "hallelujah chorus."

That's when I remembered the surgery I'd had on my vocal cords just two weeks earlier, and that I hadn't sung but a few odd notes since then. I thought: "I'm singing! God gave me my voice back, just in time to sing His praises."

Okay, I didn't go full tilt, but just about. We finished, they started the meeting, and half an hour later the group asked if we could sing the song again. This time, a colorfully dressed, rail-thin Maasai woman came over mid-song and hung a big white handmade cross around my neck. The cross, my prized possession from the trip, now hangs on the wall above my desk.

O, for a brand-new tongue to sing my great Redeemer's praise. Amazing how, when God works things together for good, it's to His glory.

Bathing in Luxury

As I related earlier, I was in Tanzania accompanying donors who are underwriting a terrific project that is equipping local Tanzanian volunteers to care for orphans and vulnerable children in their communities, as well as people living with HIV and AIDS. Overall, the trip was quite encouraging.

The following story happened before those visits, on the night we first arrived. The next dawn would bring my 55th birthday and the teeming bustle of African life outside my window.

We arrived after dark and checked into our sufficiently comfortable hotel in Arusha, Tanzania. Though the room was somewhat ramshackle by American standards, I was surprised and glad to see a Jacuzzi tub in my bathroom! I quickly decided that this was the perfect therapy for a good night's sleep after about 24 hours of continuous travel.

I eased into the warm tub with my MP3 player and Graham Greene's classic novel *The Power and the Glory*. The story is about a priest on the run during Mexico's purge of Catholicism during the 1930s. At the page where I was picking up the story, the padre has just fled to an adjacent, safer region, where he is hosted briefly by a wealthy German gentleman farmer, an outspoken but nominal Lutheran who can barely abide Catholics. On the spacious veranda overlooking his lovely grounds, the host berates the shabby priest for the way the clergy had lived lives of relative ease in the decades prior to the purge, while the masses of Catholic believers suffered in poverty. As he endures this lengthy tongue-lashing, the priest silently and penitently flagellates himself for his naïve complicity in that system, albeit over-dramatized by his host.

The pathos in that scene, masterfully painted without a shred of direct commentary, was of course the contrast between the "gentleman's" vitriolic condemnation of the disparity between priest and parishioner and his own blindness to his ease as a wealthy landowner amid the impoverishment of his laborers. It was a poignant and well-executed literary device that I savored for its skill as well as for its meaning. How easy, I thought, for the comfortable to point an accusing finger at others while oblivious to their own advantages and complicity in unjust systems.

In the next scene, the dusty priest and his wealthy host (in a setting without indoor plumbing) walk to a cool stream nearby for their outdoor bath. Here the German gentleman picks up his scolding tune once again, sniping on about poverty and disparity. Suddenly, my awareness of his hypocrisy turned in on myself. There I was taking my bath in a Jacuzzi tub, listening to relaxing music on my high-tech cell phone and reading a novel, while just outside my hotel was a nation where the median income is about $1 a day, where poverty and HIV and malaria are daily realities.

When I told my wife about my realization, she quickly pointed out that there is nothing wrong with recharging one's batteries after a long flight and before long days. I agree. Nor—dare I add—is it patently wrong to have a comfortable hotel room where one can relax and renew after daily encounters with poverty and tragedy on trips such as this one. (We also encounter more hope than one can imagine.)

Yet as I sneered at the gentleman farmer in the story for criticizing a clergyman's privilege through eyes that were blind to his own, I caught a glimpse once again of my own privilege and my blindness to it. It's not usually as stark as simply looking out one's window to see the contrast as I did the next morning; how glad we are that it isn't that easy!

Some might protest that the situations are not the same, that the privilege in this story was at the expense of others in a way that mine is not. But I've seen enough of life to admit that some have, at least in part, because others have not. And I'm one of the "haves."

I pointed my finger at the landowner even as he pointed his finger at the priest. How convenient it is to point a finger at others, to see the speck in their eye and ignore the log in one's own.

Jesus once said, "'If any one of you is without sin, let him be the first to throw a stone'" (John 8:7). Just as Mr. Greene must have planned it, my stone landed on my own head.

Surplus Blessings from Afar

My friend, Pastor Tom Theriault, just returned from Ethiopia. He called me gushing with stories, one of which touched us both. The story took place while he was visiting the World Vision project among the Afar people.

Lots of wonderful things are happening among the Afar, and Tom is a big reason why. He just made his eighth trip there in nine years to encourage the workers and people; back home, he's a tireless advocate and voice for the forgotten Afar. Clean water, health clinics, and schools are all blooming in the desert. So are food crops, thanks to agricultural training—a revolution for the pastoralist (animal-herding) Afar, who have never been farmers and are terribly vulnerable to drought and food insecurity.

Tom told me that three of these recently trained "agro-pastoralists" had just received model-farmer awards from the prime minister of Ethiopia himself. Tom and his group were able to meet two of the award recipients at their farms. He told me of one farmer who stood proudly erect, her medal draped around her neck, award certificate in hand, with a photo of her and the prime minister shaking hands. Can you imagine her pride? As an Afar, and as a woman?

Tom's group toured her fields and saw all her various crops, and then she proudly announced that her income had increased six times from what it had been before she farmed!

She now earns up to $400 per year, a staggering amount for the desperately poor Afar.

Tom asked her in his ever-enthusiastic, lyrical voice, "So what did you do with all this extra money?" They were hoping to hear about how she is improving her home and is better able to provide for her children.

As a microenterprise junkie, I was hoping Tom might even report that she's investing it in expanding her new agribusiness.

But her reply brought the group up short—"I was able to give it to people who are in need."

Sometimes, in some places, the poor stay poor for a very simple reason: they are not willing to leave others behind. An African proverb says, "He who travels alone travels fast. He who travels with others travels far." Translation? The well-being of all takes precedence over increasing the wealth of one.

I told this story to another Afar-addicted donor who has visited there. He replied, almost in frustration, "What is it with these people? Even though they have absolutely nothing, what little they have, they give away. It's a reverse of the Scripture that says 'Even what little they have will be taken away' [Luke 19:26, NLT]. The Afar *give* it away."

Anyone in my line of work knows there are two edges to that sword, that an ambitious individual can be held back by others in the extended family or clan who want or even demand a generous sharing of the newfound wealth for any and all claimants. I'm sure it's a difficult balance for many like this woman.

Yet I think we've lost something in our everyone-for-himself worldview, something that the Afar know only too well: we have no real title to our possessions. I think our worldview partly explains why preachers have to spend so much energy convincing us to cough up even a 10-percent offering to God. We might cheerily proclaim with Scripture, "Everything we have comes from you, Lord." But the rest of that verse rams into our private ownership paradigm: "We have given you only what comes from your hand" (1 Chronicles 29:14). All we're doing is giving back what is rightfully God's anyway, what we've been given from God's hand, from His blessing.

This humble Muslim Afar woman, working her fingers to the bone to eke out $400 a year, seems to understand the biblical paradigm of generosity better than I do. At least, she seems to more easily live it out. She doesn't just eat out of God's generous hand; she shares with others what she finds there.

For All Who Are Thirsty

As usual these days, we arrived late at our Episcopal church, just as the procession was starting. Which of course on this Easter Sunday meant that the only open seats were on the front row of the side chapel. What we didn't expect is that we'd have the best seats in the house.

About five feet away, off the end of the front rows of the main seating facing the altar, was a woman sitting in a wheelchair that was clearly *not* temporary. Yet she sang out joyfully, wearing a smile that matched the brightness of her dress. Occasionally her son, a happy boy with Down syndrome, scrambled over other adult laps down the row to rest on hers.

It was especially moving to watch everyone come to the altar for communion. We might have expected an Easter parade of "beautiful people," but instead the woman in the wheelchair was just the first of the lame and the infirm, some leaning on canes, others sitting in wheelchairs, with the rest of us humbly on our knees, hands outstretched to take hold of the broken body of Christ, the Bread of Life, necks craned to receive the cup of salvation.

Suddenly my eyes were opened. These people were dressed in their Easter finery not out of pretense but as part of their act of worship. No one was attired so gloriously as to be above the humility of bended knee, outstretched and supplicating hands, hungry as baby birds in the nest for what gifts Jesus had to give us.

A little boy, maybe 3 years old, was hungry too; he wouldn't let the cup pass him by without getting a drink. Other children came forward, as they come every week here, as Jesus bade them come, to receive a blessing upon their heads or to experience the communion mystery they yet hardly understand; which, after all, is true for all of us. Maybe children understand with their hearts more than we understand with our heads.

Every week there's a cacophony of comings and goings at the altar that I simply can't tear my eyes from. Today it was multiplied into a banquet feast, Father John moving from end to end and back again, giving the bread to every supplicant, trailed by four lay leaders providing wine.

The rhythm of broken, "imperfect" bodies coming forward, punctuating the pageantry, was stunning. I thought of Bob Cratchit's report to his wife in Dickens' *A Christmas Carol* about Tiny Tim's comment on Christmas morning: "He told me, coming home, that he hoped the people saw him in the church, because he was a cripple, and it might be pleasant to them to remember ... who made lame beggars walk, and blind men see." Here they came, their outward condition the only visible suggestion that their want of God's touch was any different than my own. And what a seat I had to look upon them.

In the last group to the altar, a man at the communion rail struggled to hold the wafer, almost hiding it in his fists. A kindly, knowing lay minister extracted the wafer and dipped it in the chalice, then placed it on the man's tongue, touching him compassionately on his shoulder. Only when the man arose did I see his cane, his uncertain gait, and his withered hands.

And as he traveled slowly back up the side aisle between me and the lady in the wheelchair, her happy son playing peacefully, my eyes suddenly grew moist.

"As he went along, [Jesus] saw a man blind from birth. His disciples asked him, 'Rabbi, who sinned, this man or his parents, that he was born blind?' 'Neither this man nor his parents sinned,' said Jesus, 'but this happened so that the work of God might be displayed in his life'" (John 9:1-3).

What a celebration of the work of God I was privileged to partake in this Easter Day—a celebration not only of the historical event, but of the tableau He displayed before me: all of us imperfect, all of us needy, hungry, and thirsty at the foot of the empty cross.

The Great Inspiration

Election Day 2008 found me hosting a group of 10 visitors for a one-day trip to Tijuana, where once again we visited the poorest squatter slums, met amazing people, and witnessed their pride in their businesses—as well as their outreach efforts.

While meeting the microbusiness operators is always inspiring, what moved me most on this trip was hearing from a cohort of volunteers who told us about the many wonderful things they are doing to improve their communities. Our discussion started slowly. Eliana, the first volunteer to speak, seemed rather tentative. But she warmed up as she explained her work training children in biblical values. She told how, when she realized that many came without eating, she began feeding these undernourished kids with her own food. Soon other volunteers were pitching in to help and more resources were being added. As she told her story, her enthusiasm and commitment started a crescendo of energetic pride that grew with each volunteer's report.

The last to speak, Maria, recounted how she'd organized a boys' *futbol* (soccer) team, although when she started, she knew nothing about playing the sport. The new team lost every game miserably at first, but slowly the boys gained skill and respect and started winning. Now Maria has organized a girls' team too. But I think she is the biggest winner. This woman with a third-grade education spoke to us with head high, eyes wide, and infectious love for these kids spilling over.

Crammed between these bookends were a dozen other women, all volunteers, all passionately responding to needs in their own communities, building lives and sewing bedspreads (which they proudly displayed) to increase their families' incomes. But more importantly, sewing a neighborhood out of a slum—each woman a patchwork piece of the strengthening social fabric of her community.

Two days later, after the historic U.S. election of the first person of color to the nation's highest office, I arrived in Washington, D.C. What a stimulating time to be in the nation's capital, regardless of how one voted. Plaudits were gushing in from all over the world, foreign writers hailing the return of the American Dream, re-invigorated with fresh evidence that here, anyone can grow up to do anything.

I was there to host a small conference of microfinance supporters from around the country for a weekend gathering, which was held in the historic Willard Hotel on Pennsylvania Avenue, just two blocks from the White House. Abraham Lincoln had stayed for a month on the property preparing his cabinet; the term *lobbyist* was coined from jaw-boning with presidents in the hotel lobby; and Martin Luther King Jr. put the finishing touches on "I Have a Dream" while staying at the Willard the night before his historic delivery of the speech.

Saturday at dusk, after our event ended, I strolled to the White House south lawn gate. Autumn leaves framed the facade and grounds. I found myself standing next to an older African-American couple who were gazing in silence at the White House, holding hands. I couldn't help but wonder, "What must be going through their minds?" I decided not to disturb their meditations (prayers? thanksgiving? angst?) but felt some solidarity in standing peacefully next to them as we watched history change along with the unusually balmy November evening's light.

Later I sat alone at a sidewalk bistro reading a fascinating book, *Hard Times: An Oral History of the Great Depression* by Studs Terkel. A friend had passed along the book. It had seemed to put some palpable fear of our own economic future into him, so I was not at all sure I wanted to subject myself to it! But the prior night I'd cracked it open and the very first accounts hooked me. I read about the Bonus Boys,

World War I veterans who were out of work and out of GI benefits and who marched on Washington to demand a bonus. Many camped out right here on Pennsylvania Avenue until Army troops under Generals MacArthur, Patton, and Eisenhower were finally called in to force the protesters out at bayonet-point from the spot where I'd stood outside the White House lawn. Historic hopes had been crushed on the spot where I'd so recently been standing with a newly hopeful couple.

Reading *Hard Times* at that sidewalk cafe was an immediate encounter with the heart of the poor. Intermixed with stories of great hardship and pain were accounts of great compassion and inspiration. I felt the same way many people feel who visit an impoverished country and return saying, "I fully expected to see the poverty, but I didn't expect to witness so much hope, so much joy and generosity."

Somehow these accounts of compassion and love in the midst of those hard times gave me a glimpse of our own nation's historic social fabric, albeit of a bygone and nearly forgotten era. Here are a few samples:

Kitty: "There were many beggars, who would come to your back door, and they would say they were hungry. I wouldn't give them money because I didn't have it. But I did take them in my kitchen and give them something to eat ... I gave him a good, warm meal."

Pauline: "My neighbors were angry with my mother, because she fed hungry men at the back door. They said it would bring others, and then what would she do? She said, 'I'll feed them till the food runs out.'"

Emma: "Sometimes we would see them on the railroad tracks pickin' up stuff, and we would tell 'em: 'Come to our house.' They would come by and we would give 'em an old shirt or a pair of pants or some old shoes. We would always give 'em food."

These 1933 realities seem so foreign to our 2008 sensibilities, a mere 75 years later. Housewives taking unknown, hungry men into their kitchens? What about safety? What about fear? For those quoted above and many others, there was a sense that

We are all in this together; we are all of a piece
I have something you need more than we do
So here's my husband's suit
And some nice, warm food
I've heated it just for you
Instead of calling the police

One of our speakers in D.C. had reminded us that God not only loves but also bestows dignity upon the poor, and that His economy works only if we expect the best from them: integrity, repayment, industry, dignity. I sensed those very expectations in the preceding quotes.

I was overwhelmed by these stories. I recognized an ethic of mutuality that I thought was too dissonant with our rugged individualism to be an American attribute, rather something other cultures had and from which we could only hope to learn. But it turns out that we may only need to re-learn it. Glory to God!

And depending on the direction our economy takes in the days ahead, we may be compelled to re-learn it.

I'm understanding more about Africa and more about the mindset of the poor in general by reading a book of quotes from erstwhile middle-class Americans who "lost everything" in the Great Depression; yet maybe they gained the real treasure.

"'For what will it profit a man if he gains the whole world and forfeits his soul?'" Jesus asked then and asks now (Matthew 16:26, NASB). Last week, I glimpsed the same vibrant soul in the squatter slums of Tijuana as I did in the intertwined stories of survival during America's Great Depression. Lives woven together in mutual support create the true social fabric of every community, whether the size of a neighborhood or a globe, and may best reflect the community Jesus describes as the kingdom of heaven.

Over-Due Diligence

My pastor, Father John Taylor, was leading a small Bible study last week. We were talking about Jesus' radical call to love. Father John suddenly asked our little band if we would hear his "confession" on this topic.

He preceded his story with the comment that every pastor knows when he or she takes the job that they will be hoodwinked and taken advantage of somewhere along the way. They understand it's part of the package in their calling.

Then he proceeded to tell us a story only five hours old, of how he'd been working busily away when a stranger came to the church office and asked to speak to him. The man told a woeful story about needing medications that very day and of how he "needed about $70 to buy these medicines, but you can call Pastor So-and-so in Louisiana who knows me and can vouch for me."

So Father John actually called Pastor So-and-so. When he reached him, the voice on the phone said, "Yes, I know this man and his situation, though to be truthful he's something of a user of the church's benevolence. But he may well need these medications due to some real health problems."

Like others of us faced with the anguish of such a choice, I think Father John feels that a worse option than being taken advantage of is to say no to Jesus, who, in Mother Teresa's words, often comes to us "in the distressing disguise of the poor."

So, in the wake of the informative but ultimately un-illuminating report from his fellow clergyman, Father John decided to take time out of his day and go to a local drugstore with the prescriptions to purchase this petitioner's medications.

As it turns out, that particular drugstore had only one of the two needed medications in stock; the other drug would have to be purchased at another store. By the time he received this joyous news, Father John realized he had already spent far too much time and energy trying to be both an ambassador of Christ and a wise steward of church funds. He did not have time for more. And if he couldn't get a receipt by purchasing the medication himself, he didn't feel right using church funds.

So he came to the conclusion (rather painful on his pastor's salary) that the only financial option was to give the solicitor $70 of his own money. He went into a store to use an ATM, but of course it was broken. More time, more hassle ... but he finally obtained the $70. By this time he had anything but love in his heart.

He marched up to the man, handed him the $70, and said in a rather stern voice, "This is a loan. I want to get my money back. You are an able-bodied person and I expect you to earn enough to repay me. And then repay the church in Louisiana!"

Of course, this was a lose-lose situation; neither party felt good about the transaction. And that's what it was—a business transaction gone south, which in this case could stand for "sour in the mouth."

Father John wanted to confess his cantankerous attitude to us, though our group as a whole would have nothing of it. Surely he'd gone beyond the call of Christian duty for this man, the group protested.

But I knew what he was lamenting: God dearly loves a cheerful giver, and there was no joy in Mudville today. Certainly, this was not the ideal story of gleeful generosity.

I looked around the circle and realized there were seven of us. I did the math and excitedly plotted for a moment to suggest we all throw in $10 to share this burden with our padre! But cheerful giving rarely works that way. Someone always jumps in the deep end, others in the shallow end, and some don't want to get wet at all.

Instead, I did what I really felt in my gut like doing: I slipped twenty bucks into his Bible when he wasn't looking. (I've since made my own confession to him, but I knew if I'd tried to hand him the money that evening he wouldn't understand my motives or accept the money.)

I didn't give him the money out of pity, not in the least. I'd just returned a few days earlier from Ethiopia. Because of where we were in the capital, Addis Ababa, we had encountered more beggars than on any previous visit. I gave to some but not to others. It was all quite unsettling, yet the only thing worse than running those beggars' gauntlets would have been to avoid them and their needs in order to keep from feeling distressed.

All told, if I gave away even $10 in appropriately small *birr* bills and coins, I'd be surprised. Then I came home, where I'm as insulated as my neighbors from beggars, save the increasingly rare person I see on the street corner as I wait at a traffic light, trying to decide how much eye contact I can give them and whether to roll down a window. Dare I care?

But pastors like Father John are not as insulated. For them, it comes with the territory. Sap that I am, I continue to feel it's a beautiful thing that the poor come to the houses of God for help. They congregated around the Orthodox cathedral in Addis, and they still come to our churches.

No, I gave Father John the $20 because I wanted a piece of the action. He had already conducted more due diligence than I ever would or could. He's far more adept at dealing with situations and people like this. Yes, he'll likely never be repaid, but I want to be in on his investor pool in that situation. For a measly $20, he became my agent and I got to participate in his act of goodwill (imperfect as such acts always are).

As I left, I laughed at myself. I tell donors all the time that they can be powerful voices for the poor after they've visited a project or have a history of engagement with a nonprofit: "There are people in your sphere of influence who respect you," I say, "and you've had a chance to do the due diligence they can't do. So if you let them know you've checked it out, there's a good chance they'll invest too."

I guess I proved to myself the veracity of my coaching. Well, at a $20 level anyway.

I could have evenly split the $70 investment cost with Father John. But, master preacher that he is, I expect he'll get a good sermon illustration out of the story somewhere down the road, and that's probably worth his fifty bucks.

Beauty and the Beach

I had an all-round lovely day today. I hosted some entrepreneur donors on a visit to projects outside Tijuana. All of us were very encouraged by our time there.

I hadn't been to the Pedregal community in the past year but carried vivid memories of hovels built on the trash-heaped hillside, as did some of the returning visitors. But when we arrived, we were amazed at how many permanent housing improvements the community members were making. Cinder-block walls seemed to be going up all around.

I remember a visit to Guatemala a few years earlier, when we met a humble woman who was operating her own weaving business thanks to a microcredit loan she'd received. A big stack of cinder blocks stood to the side of her home. The woman told us that each time she saves sufficient profits from her business, she patiently purchases 100 more blocks. As we could see, the family was ever-so-gradually replacing each tin-sheeted wall in their home with these sturdy substitutes, wall by wall, and replacing their dirt floor with concrete. Such structural changes to a home can dramatically reduce the incidence of childhood illnesses, and they reduce the vulnerability of the poor to hurricanes, storms, and earthquakes.

In the squatter settlements around Tijuana, housing improvements like these may also be the best measure of the level of hope in a community, hope that people can stay and make a life and won't be bulldozed away, hope that the municipal government will care for them instead of harass them, hope for their future. Turning a ramshackle, plywood shack into a cinder-block-and-stucco home is a huge investment: one that poor-yet-wise people only make as they feel it's safe to put down roots, to stake a claim, both indicating a desire to reduce their vulnerability and reflecting an already-reduced vulnerability. So this was a big deal.

One visitor had brought his 10-year-old granddaughter, Becca, who bounced in the back of the van as we drove back to the border. I asked Becca what she would remember most from the day. She told me she'd remember playing ball with two boys. "But it wasn't the playing, really. It was seeing that they were happy, even though they were so poor. They were happy anyway, for what they have. That was really something." Out of the mouths of babes.

Back at the border, we all hugged and went our separate ways. I was just in time for rush hour on the interstate, so I took the beach highway instead, thinking I might stop at some point and take a refreshing ocean swim. I chickened out in the end (thankfully, because 36 hours later a swimmer was killed by a shark nearby), but in the meantime I saw something like an apparition.

As the low sun's glare and the springtime wind both bounced off the ocean toward me, there on the sparsely populated beach was a young woman and a hula hoop. I'd never seen this kind of acrobatics before, but she could move the hoop anywhere she wanted with the slightest hip-pop or sway. The hoop obeyed each command her movements gave it; traveling down from a hand high above her head to her neck, around her knees, then back around one arm, then spinning one way as she spun herself around and around in the other direction, the hoop now down around one knee while the other leg extended in an arabesque, then the hoop vertically spinning on her shoulders while she leaned over horizontally. On and on. Such a fluid motion. She made it look easy and relaxing, though I'm sure I'd be either defeated in 10 seconds or exhausted in 30. She must have been in good shape, though her blousy shirt and jeans and the distance at which I stood made it hard to tell for sure.

This was art. Her body and the hoop were one. The sunlight sparkled off the choppy lines of surf behind her; the wind was in my face. It was a beautiful experience.

At first she seemed showy, but there was only a handful of people around and, for some reason, no one seemed to pay her much attention. I wish someone had officially announced her performance so I wouldn't have felt self-conscious watching, as though I were gawking. I wish I'd paid more attention instead of talking to the lifeguard up on the sandbank, still thinking about swimming and only furtively glancing at her, marveling each time and momentarily losing myself in the art. There was a show on display here, a conspiracy of dancing sunlight and dancing woman-lithe, a dance of earth, wind, woman, and sea.

I finally slipped off my shoes and walked down to the surf's edge where she was dancing and circling and swaying, making music with a hula hoop. I knew I could watch her more clearly from there without the sun's glare. Of course, that's the very moment when she packed up and left.

Just as well. Some sights are better from a distance.

From a distance she seemed like a tiny dancer, free as the wind in my face, celebrating unhindered freedom, expression, and maybe even hope. In her sun dance, the woman and the sun and the wind and the sand all seemed to cooperate in prophesying the same future of freedom and hope that we saw being mixed into the cement of each new cinder-block wall in Pedregal. I pictured in the eyes of my heart the people there unhindered too, free to express, create, build, and become anything. The woman on the beach, like a snake charmer, was calling out the fullness packed into my heart.

God has a future and a hope for our Pedregal friends; He knows what it is. But it's difficult for us to visualize their future. It's elusive, something seen only from a distance, through a glass dimly. Just as the dancer moved when I attempted to see her better, our vision of Pedregal's future somehow moves away when we try to examine it. But at a distance, it beckons; and even the beckoning is a delight and a celebration, a perfect final act to the day.

Representative Poverty

I finally saw a beggar in my little town last Saturday, or at least I think I did. He was the first I've seen in several years, and he seemed so out of place it was almost surreal.

He was a little old man with very dark skin. A walking stick rested beside him. He sat hunched like Jonah in the dark shadow of one of those singular trees artificially plopped into the parking lots of sunny suburban strip malls. It was so odd, as though he'd been transported from my memories of traveling the urban streets in Bangladesh or India.

I was glad to see him. It's not that I enjoy seeing beggars or that I'm happy some people feel they have to beg. Rather, my town and I need to be reminded that there are people like him all over the world. This man with his bony-legged squat, south-Asian skin color, walking stick, and lack of English seemed like an apparition and a representative of all those others, as though he'd been sent there just for us. For me.

I mooched something from Janet's purse to give him, but when he reached out to receive it, his hands didn't seem to work properly. Perhaps that was part of his shtick. No matter; I tend to be a bit of a sucker for folks like this.

While we walked past the beggars in Addis Ababa earlier this year, I told my traveling companions a story to explain my unsophisticated but strongly held actions and philosophy on giving alms.

It was 1984, and I was preparing for my first-ever Vision Trip, heading to India. Back then, traveling to visit projects among the poor was much more rare. Our group gathered from several cities at the Los Angeles International Airport to receive an official orientation from a seasoned traveler before our international flight. One point he made very clear was that we should never give money to beggars. He told us many compelling reasons for this: not putting ourselves at risk, not being taken advantage of, not encouraging begging as a profession.

On our very first day in India, after a hair-raising journey to the hotel from the Madras (now Chennai) airport—which evoked images from the song *Marrakesh Express*—and then a poor night's sleep, we met some wonderful local staff and went to see our first project. Afterward, we headed back to the van, already chock-full of feelings from our project visit. Several beggars approached us in a swarm, each with one hand outstretched and the other tapping his or her mouth. Their mournful eyes spoke words that we didn't need to understand in order to comprehend. I was so glad for the clear instruction we'd received at LAX, for being relieved of the guilt, the complexity, and the need for discernment, and spared the possible trickery of the beggars.

We all piled into the shabby van as fast as we possibly could, trying to look away when these unwelcome solicitors came to the windows (which were thankfully locked), petitioning us now more fervently as their opportunity slipped away. To our relief, one by one they slowly gave up and moved away as the driver started the engine and put the vehicle in gear. Eventually, only one remained.

She was a sight I don't believe I've ever seen before or since, a woman with no nose on her face, no fingers on her hands. She was so visually repulsive that she was frightening. She gently thumped her fingerless palms together, tipping her head to one side, pleading. Pleading in a professional way, to be certain. There were no tears; she'd done this before.

I was experiencing such drastic culture shock already, this was more than I could stand to watch. I turned away again.

Just then, as we started to pull out into the street, our Indian host—a World Vision colleague—unlocked a window and slid it open just a crack. Into her palms he placed some of his own money. She bowed multiple times in thanksgiving.

I was shocked! I had followed the clear rules of engagement we'd been given, with arguments that all made so much sense back home amid the glass walls and jumbo jets. How could he do this? Didn't he know the dangers?

Certainly he knew, Nirmal told us. You have to be careful, you have to be discreet, and your timing should be considered. "But how could I, as a Christian, not respond?" he asked in turn. "Did you see her?"

No, maybe I didn't see her. I saw what was missing, what scared me; maybe I didn't see what remained—her humanity.

More than shock, I felt cheated. As the initial revulsion and fear subsided and her humanity came into my consciousness, I realized that only dear Nirmal had experienced the blessing of representing to her the One who touched the lepers.

I was busy following rules; he was following his heart and his faith commitment. I was following some well-intentioned guidelines proffered by Christians; Nirmal showed us all how to respond like Christ Himself, the One who called us to reach beyond rules and laws and appropriately apply the overarching law of love, of compassion first.

We often say that we want Vision Trips to be transformational experiences. Sometimes, maybe most of the time, transformation cannot be programmed. It's not on the day's schedule; it's not something you can check off a list.

That day at a dusty, graveled curb, between the scheduled project visits, I had an unplanned experience that is forever burned into my memory as though it happened yesterday.

This is why I often give to beggars. Not to encourage them, but to identify with them, to acknowledge their humanity, to look them in the eyes hoping they will look back at mine and not look down, the look-away of shame.

That fingerless, noseless woman represented millions more like her, and reminded me of the humanity we all share. The few coins she didn't receive from me have been multiplied many times over to others, not as penance but freely given. I don't always let my head overrule my heart anymore, lest I miss the chance to "see" someone. Someone in the shadows, keeping his distance, looking as lonely as the half-grown tree in a sea of asphalt under which he sits.

I didn't want to make the same mistake again.

Mining Olympic Gold

The latest World Vision magazine came last week. A vulnerable child is pictured on the cover, over the title "Comfort in CRISIS." I cringe a little each time I look at it. Truthfully, I haven't yet been able to bring myself to read it.

In contrast, the opening ceremony for the 2008 Summer Olympics in Beijing took place last Friday evening. I only stumbled onto the live TV coverage by chance, but I ended up watching almost every moment of the compellingly gorgeous display. Even the slow procession of national teams arrayed in brightly colored ethnic clothing was difficult not to watch.

Here was God's diversity on display, a sumptuous banquet of international brotherhood, youthful vigor, and excellence. The pinnacle of humanity and mankind's achievement. As soon as we flipped on the opening ceremony, it was just as Renée Zellweger's character admits in the movie "Jerry McGuire": "You had me at 'hello.'"

There is something inviting about the Olympics, in contrast to what I felt about the World Vision magazine cover. They are like two books, one entitled Good News, the other entitled Bad News.

At times it takes courage to pick up bad news and read it. Kay Warren did that five years ago when *Time* magazine published a cover story about the global AIDS pandemic, and her entire life's trajectory has changed since then. Now the current issue of *Time* features Kay's husband Rick on the cover and a story highlighting their church's work in Rwanda. Much of the impetus for that work initially came out of Kay's passion about AIDS. Bad news has that power, when we're willing to open ourselves to it.

Yet it takes courage to do so. I am privileged to know a number of women living in Orange County's high-priced beach cities who have organized a book club devoted solely to reading about issues of poverty, the global plight of girls and women, and children in crisis. When we've all spent so much energy creating our safe, comfortable cloisters away from the suffering of the teeming masses, it seems crazy that these women would open themselves to such depressing topics. And heroic.

I guess I do the same thing. When I think of it that way, it seems the farthest thing from insane. In fact, it's what keeps me sane in a world where these realities are far more prevalent than my man-made, theme-park world.

I saw solemnity in Janet's eyes this morning. She's reading a riveting book about the challenges faced by women and girls around the world, and last night's chapter about rape as an instrument of war hung over her like the low clouds outside our window.

I suppose misery loves company. I was the one who commended the book to her when I finished it, and I took real comfort from her disconcerted feelings. Because I get up every day, in spite of it all. And so should she. I sing barbershop love songs. I play oldies music with friends on Friday evenings down the canyon from our town. And I do all of it while carrying around a fairly keen understanding of the suffering and plight of the have-nots. If I wanted to prove a point, I might even sing Louis Armstrong's "What a Wonderful World," because it is. The same world produces music, gang rape, butterflies, children, smiles, famine. And the diversity of all of it is displayed in the Olympic ceremonies.

Yes, there is a darker story, and it takes courage to embrace that reality. But in doing just that, we find that our hallelujahs, while perhaps quieter and less demonstrative, are more authentic, more honest.

For many years, I kept on hand an article written in the late 1980s by a World Vision employee who helped our relief staff working in disaster situations cope with the emotional toll of their work. He explained to the rest of us that these people may not be very enthusiastic in the weekly chapel meeting at headquarters, but this didn't mean they had lost their faith. Rather, he said, in a line that has haunted me ever since, "They hold onto their belief in a loving God *despite evidence to the contrary*." (Emphasis added.)

Ignoring evidence in court, just like ignoring the reality of suffering in our world and the cries behind the suffering, only leads to injustice and ignorance. And while ignorance may seem like bliss, in the end it's only yet another form of darkness.

Still, sometimes (like during the Olympics) it's nice to simply enjoy looking at the glass half-full, celebrate that half and lift it high, and enjoy its bouquet as a foretaste of a kingdom without end, of peace on earth and goodwill toward all.

Enjoying that new wine is good for the soul. It restores my courage and reminds me that the world is not all darkness. Who knows? It may even give me courage enough to pick up and read that magazine in front of me.

Seek First to Understand

It only took one look. One glance at those beautiful little girls we had just been with, as they played the games little girls play. Then every question was answered, every skeptical thought silenced.

It happened last week in Tijuana, but the questions had begun a few weeks earlier at a gathering in Orange County. That evening, I stood at the back of a small forest of obedient men, each paired with a wife or significant other who'd convinced them to attend. We were stuffed into a living room and kitchen overflow to hear from World Vision Mexico staff about a humble community center this group of women had helped underwrite, which the community had now built—almost entirely with their own hands.

I could tell that my colleague Mauricio sensed he needed to speak quickly as the photos cycled by on the big-screen TV behind him. My heart began to sink onto the kitchen floor as I stood behind the crowd, which was courteously quiet but had been reluctant to stop conversing and come inside for his report. How could we possibly understand, from the comfort of this lovely home and our own lives, the transforming significance of this little cinder-block shell of a community center cut into a hillside in a squatter slum on the dirty skirt-hem of Tijuana? How could we understand the sense of community identity and self-respect, the sense of "place" that it gives to these transplants from some other, poorer region who have ended up on toeholds on the sides of a canyon, hoping to begin their climb to a better life for their families?

In his report, Mauricio announced that the community now wants to build an "indoor soccer court" at the community center. Who can fault the chuckles and raised eyebrows from the listeners? We were having an informational update, not transporting ourselves into the reality of this squatter settlement. How could the attendees understand his meaning, that this dream is the even-more-humble equivalent of a gang-ridden urban neighborhood building a caged basketball court so kids don't have to play in the dangerous street?

I wanted to call out, to stop the presentation, to ask the polite listeners to transport themselves, just for a few moments. I wanted them to ask questions that could move them into the context of a vastly different reality from the one in which we now stood, into a reality just 90 miles south. That evening, it was a bridge too far.

The presentation ended. The men asked questions about safety, meaning their wives' personal safety in traveling there; there were no questions about the safety of the children who have no playground or soccer field save the trash-strewn hillsides where their homes, often made of materials otherwise destined for America's landfills, precariously stand.

A packed signup list full of women's names testified to the willingness of many to break out of our comfortable bubble and walk a mile in dusty shoes. But I felt a heaviness, especially for the men who are only annual, outside observers. I sensed that we'd missed a precious opportunity to expand our understanding of a different reality, to experience a different set of expectations and hopes and dreams.

All that changed last week when I took that group of 16 visitors to the community center. Inside, we witnessed a vocational training class for future beauticians. We learned about the amazing commitment of local volunteers who oversee health programs and scholarship programs, train their neighbors in income-generating activities, coach soccer teams for boys and girls (now with eight or nine trophies on display!), teach biblical values, hold after-school programs, and coordinate child sponsorship.

What a delight it was for half of us to meet the children we recently began sponsoring in Tijuana! Some of the women cried when they met their sponsored children for the first time, exchanged small gifts, and had a barbeque together at the center. I gave my sponsored child, 9-year-old José, a soccer jersey and a Frisbee, and we went outside to play catch with his younger brother and dad.

Some of the little girls, who had been among us, touched us, posed for our cameras, and sat in their mothers' laps during the presentations, went outside too. And in one moment, a vision which had sounded absurd a month earlier made perfect sense.

As girls everywhere do, these girls created a form of a tea party, which they played on a precarious stack of plywood jumbled up right next to a four-foot precipice that dropped off onto concrete. The platform for their game was a 5-foot-square scrap, one edge studded with nails pointing right up through the plywood. These *chicas* shuffled around a makeshift table atop the platform and kneeled or sat around it. Somehow no one fell off and no one was impaled by a nail, clean or dirty. Yet there wasn't one visitor who didn't look at those precious children and immediately, with a single glance, understand completely what they hadn't understood that evening back home in Orange County.

"Seek first to understand" is perhaps the one habit of Stephen Covey's *The 7 Habits of Highly Effective People* that haunts me the most. Nothing much of value can happen in this world without first understanding—especially understanding people.

These days, the drumbeat I hear in Scripture is God's concern for the poor, the orphan, and the widow. It catches me up in the oddest moments, like buried landmines in a field: while chanting the day's psalms during vespers at an abbey, when reading those ever-troublesome gospel words in red letters, even while slogging through the Law and the Prophets.

When I pause and actually seek to understand the words (rather than recoiling as though from a guilt-inducing scolding, or dismissing them as figures of speech), I begin to recognize the plaintive heart's cry of the biblical writers and their people as the cry of the marginalized, and I quickly choke up.

We each have many opportunities to seek understanding, to build a bridge toward those who are different from us. I miss those opportunities most of the time. But lately I'm hearing a beckoning call to understand a reality articulated throughout the ages right in my Bible, and lived daily right down Interstate 5, a reality quite different from my own. Jesus came to understand, to walk our sod, to live our life. God incarnate.

And when we seek to see through God's eyes, we too can become incarnational.

What I Can Do

You know how sometimes you start to enjoy someone and think they could be a long-term friend, and then they do or say something that crosses the invisible line and makes you think, "I am not on the same page with this person?" Well, you may decide I've just crossed your line.

Let me explain. Last week, *The Economist* reported that people in El Salvador are eating only half of what they ate just one year ago. Of course, the Salvadorans to which this article refers are the poorest, the already vulnerable, the habitually hungry, the ones who cannot make up the cost difference in the face of the recent rise in food prices. In other words, they are the least able to survive on half the food.

I've thought of that statistic often this past week, and I've really been burdened by the growing global food crisis. I read several articles about the causes and impacts of this problem and watched a moving video clip from the *Washington Post* website, which ran a weeklong series on the crisis.

A few days ago it struck me that, in America, this whole food crisis idea seems like a phantom that has no substance in my world and no impact on those nearest to me. By now, I completely believe the crisis is real, but I don't personally feel it. And therefore it doesn't change me or my decisions. In effect, I am unknowingly outbidding hungry slum dwellers for foodstuffs that I may well throw away, because I can afford to pay higher prices than they can pay. And in the process, I deprive them of their daily bread. The same daily bread that I'm praying God will give them.

Honestly, I love abundance thinking: Let's make the pie bigger so more can eat from it. And I hate scarcity thinking. But until supply catches up to demand and the markets settle down (which will reportedly take a couple of years), this will be one of those situations we all hate, where one person's consumption affects another person's ability to consume. I can pray that God will meet their needs as well as mine, but if it doesn't impact my decisions about consumption, then my prayers have a wooden ring.

Still, as I prayed for those affected, I asked God and myself: What can one person do? It's absurd to think I can personally make a measurable impact on a global problem. It's true, I can only put my one oar in the water. But often, because of this reasoning, we never do anything, never change anything. After all, I'm just one person.

But ultimately, I fear that I'm simply finding rationalizations for upholding my own status quo. This is simply not an acceptable conclusion to the matter for me right now. In fact, it's an even more unacceptable conclusion than doing something that has no real impact, because I've come to sense a deeper yearning within me, beyond my normal fix-it response: a desire to simply be in solidarity with those who suffer. For their sake, and for mine. "Weep with those who weep," Jesus said (Romans 12:15, NASB). Not "weep *for* them." "With" is the real action word in Jesus' admonition.

How could I bring this truth home and attempt in some feeble way to stand in solidarity with the hungry? Well, I could consume less. We hear a lot about reducing our carbon footprint these days. How about my food-print?

The truth is, the absolutely least-qualified people are cutting their food consumption right now because they have no choice. Those of us who would probably be healthier anyway by doing so don't have the financial need to cut ours.

A revelation: I realized I could reduce my food consumption 5 percent just by skipping one meal out of 21 each week!

So, I've decided to skip weekday lunches whenever I'm not having a work-related lunchtime meeting. I've done it four days now and if anything, I feel better. Empowered, maybe. I am more content because I'm doing something tangible, something even slightly sacrificial. Solidarity.

I know. It's benign, maybe foolish. It won't change a single statistic in any newspaper. Of course, wouldn't it be great if 1 million Americans skipped one meal a week? That could change something.

But this isn't a movement; it's just me, Cory, deciding that symbolic solidarity is a worthy end in itself, and that it trumps all the rationalizations for maintaining my status quo lifestyle while mothers in Mauritania sell their bodies for a two-pound bag of corn, and families who previously had tea and bread for breakfast and lunch can only afford the tea because I'm willing to pay more for their bread.

So for awhile, I'm going to try this, try to concentrate more on eating simply so that others might simply eat. And then I'll enjoy a party every so often. Once, God's provision was as obvious as the manna on the ground each morning. In that divinely supplied economy, those who had much never had too much, and those who had little never had too little. I think His kingdom is supposed to reflect His economy, and I want to play my small part in that.

Usually I wouldn't tell people when I'm fasting (per Jesus' admonition), but in this case, it's not mainly a spiritual discipline. It's an attempt to actually leave a few more crumbs on my table for the poor. Like the gleanings Boaz beautifully left in his fields for Ruth, out of love and compassion.

Yet in another way, this is a very spiritual undertaking, one that will no doubt recruit the help of my stomach in reminding me to pray for the hungry.

It's a risk to tell others about this decision, especially when I've only just made it. Lots could change. Maybe I'll decide next week that it's too tough, that it's keeping me from doing my work of raising money to help those very people in need. That's possible.

It's also quite possible I will revise my plan, skipping desserts instead of lunch, or any number of variations. All I know is that I feel the need to do something, and if I share my plan with others, I'm more likely to keep doing something—if only because I fear someone will ask me about it.

And maybe in the telling, someone else will see the connection between their own consumption and another person's need, and they too will consider taking a pin to our bubble of unreality that so effectively keeps us from truly feeling the pain of the have-nots.

School Fees and Fabrics

The first paragraph of the article brought me up short: "Rilato Nare was in a panic. Her children had come home far too early from their first day of school. Her son Ayanda, 12, says the school's headmaster called him and his siblings aside at midday. 'He told us to go home and not to come back until we could pay school fees. Then he prayed for us.'"

How many glimpses into the life of Africa's rural poor are packed into that one paragraph from the cover story of the Spring 2008 World Vision magazine.

School fees? Kids so poor they can't afford shoes, and yet they have to pay for schooling? It's true in many places, and it's the kids who most need a road out of desperation who can't take that road because they can't pay the toll to travel it.

Who put school fees in place? This seems to have been one of the clearer and more tangible sins of colonialism, and of well-meaning but out-of-touch World Bank–type economists who took "economically sustainable governing" to include paying tuition for public schooling—a level few would now consider fair.

Turns out all of us benefit from some subsidies in life. Except these kids who need it most. As much as I believe in economic sustainability and paying one's own way, I catch myself when the consequences of those principled proclamations of mine cause the most vulnerable to suffer things I won't have to suffer. After all, what did 12-year-old Ayanda do to deserve his fate? Nothing, besides having been born where he was born—something none of us can choose.

The schoolmaster, having perhaps already crammed in as many non-paying students as possible, can't help one more and must send

Rilato's children away.

But even in this secular school setting, his African heart and sensibility won't do so without stopping to pray for these children, to pray that God would provide the tuition money and that they would be able to come back to school. By praying, he let them know the school's door is as wide open for them as is his heart.

"He told us to go home, then he prayed for us." In a place of nothing-to-go-round except love and compassion, the schoolmaster shares generously. It's beautiful, full of pathos.

Can't the rest of us do better than simply sigh at the story? Can't I question again my own economic theories and the hardened principles that make so much sense in a glass-enclosed corporate office away from the reality of Rilato and her children's headmaster, away from the fray?

What hasn't completely frayed yet is the social fabric of a continent where neighbor-love may be the most plentiful commodity. What a pity that Africa's most precious export can't be traded for the goods and services it so desperately needs. Would that we were willing to pay generously for such a valuable fabric.

Skepticals and Spectacles

I have a confession: One of my well-loved traditions each Christmas is to watch "Mr. Magoo's Christmas Carol." Despite being no more than an animated TV special from the 1960s, it's actually a nice retelling of Dickens' classic tale, complete with tender musical numbers, with Mr. Magoo of course playing the role of Ebenezer Scrooge. In a nod to Magoo's character, the show adds his trademark squinting and unwillingness to buy himself eyeglasses. At one point, some businessmen in town say rather pompously, "So, you're the one they say is too cheap to buy himself spectacles."

Mr. Magoo would rather remain nearsighted than pay the price to see. I'm a bit like him.

For many years I've kept a quote nearby from Frederick Faber, written 150 years ago:

"The habit of judging is so nearly incurable, and its cure is such an almost interminable process, that we must concentrate ourselves for a long while on keeping it in check, and this check is to be found in kind interpretations. We must come to esteem very lightly our sharp eye for evil, on which perhaps we once prided ourselves as cleverness. We must look at our talent for analysis of character as a dreadful possibility of huge uncharitableness. We are sure to continue to say clever things, so long as we continue to indulge in this analysis; and clever things are equally sure to be sharp and acid. We must grow to something higher, and something truer, than a quickness in detecting evil" (as found in *Joy and Strength* by Mary Wilder Titleston).

I rather pride myself at times on "a quickness in detecting evil." I'm certainly not alone. A common encounter for me—it comes with the territory, I suppose—is when someone says, with a tone inviting me to confess the real story, "Come on, so how does this child sponsorship thing really work? They claim you're connected to a specific child, but that's like 4 million different children. They must just have a few thousand photos, and the money goes into a big bucket for all the kids, right? People can feel connected to a specific child, but surely that's not the way it really works."

On a trip to Malawi a few years ago, I discovered that the club of skeptics and "evil-detectives" is truly worldwide.

I accompanied a group to visit a project their church was supporting generously. This remote project covered a large geographic area, and the visitors sponsored about 20 children between them. We had to split up into three vehicles and crisscross the terrain for an entire day so the sponsors could meet the children in their home villages.

I tagged along with an American family who sponsored five or six children, so that's how many villages we traveled to, over dirt roads and foot trails. At each stop, a group of 20 to 50 villagers waited to greet us. We would start with an official gathering, then find out how many children overall were sponsored there. We would meet the American family's sponsored child along with the child's parents and siblings, if any, and see the humble mud-and-wattle home where the child lived. It was a powerful, swiftly moving day that still plays in my mind like an endearing home movie on fast-forward.

The government of Malawi has wisely incorporated its ancient network of chiefs and elders, called "traditional authorities," into its civil administration. The chiefs still retain various duties and powers in providing watchful care for their village or region.

In each village, the people would gather and we would first be greeted with a speech from the local village chief. That's where the Skeptics Club membership grew.

More than once that day, a chief said to us, "It's so good that you've come. We've heard from World Vision that there really are people in America who sponsor our children here. But we've never met any of them before now, and until today we wondered if it was really true!"

No one was going to pull the wool over their eyes!

The American family would at some point bring out a photo of the sponsored child that they'd received in the mail, and the sponsored child invariably brought along a photo the sponsors had mailed to him or her. The faces in the photos would indeed match the faces of the parties standing there, and everyone would laugh at our shared skeptical tendencies.

I love to tell that story when Americans ask me the question about sponsorship, because each one of us somehow fancies that we are especially clever and, well, while all the other donors might be suckers, "I'm different." I told a friend the story and she replied, "Wow, that's like looking into a mirror, a foreign mirror, but seeing yourself."

Now, no one wants to be duped. But here's the rub: Somehow we equate skepticism with intelligence. I'm smart enough that I can make sure I won't be cheated, we tell ourselves. Yet as soon as we construct that equation, we are well on our way to the "dreadful possibility of huge uncharitableness," in our judgments and words, that Faber wrote about and that I see in myself.

Magoo's Scrooge was such a skeptic. Scrooge's nearsightedness allowed him to stay in his comfortable world of judgment and cynicism until his divine appointment with the spirits showed him another world, a world of kinder interpretations.

That's the world I strive to live in, with many failures strewn along the way.

Lord, grant me less fear of being duped and more fear of being unkind, acidic, and uncharitable in my interpretations. Grant me spectacles to see beyond my comfortable judgments and skepticism. Help me grow "to something higher, and something truer, than a quickness in detecting evil."

Turning the Tables

It's amazing who you can track down on Google these days. Me, for instance.

That's right. I got an e-mail last month entitled "To Your Surprise" from a guy I met once, in 1984, while in rural India. He's a former World Vision India staffer, and we spent three hair-raising days together visiting projects and trying not to die on the roads of Kerala, a state on the southwestern tip of that lovely country. I probably wrote him a letter afterward, but we've not been in touch for a quarter-century.

Yet here was his e-mail saying that he left World Vision a few years ago and became a full-time evangelist, and he's just about to embark on a trip to pray in all 50 of these United States. He'll be coming to California, he found me on Google, and he would love to see me and tell me more. Gulp.

Then today I got a phone message from a voice I could barely understand. "Yes brother, we are here in . . ." He turns away from the phone. "Where are we now?" he asks someone nearby. "Oh yes, I'm in California. We are here only until tomorrow night and then we fly to Hawaii and Alaska. I would love to see you before I go!"

I don't know what thoughts go through your mind when you hear that an evangelist from a poor country feels called to travel far more extensively through America than you ever have, but I had many sorts of thoughts. One thought I didn't have was, "Lord, I'm sure glad someone came here from half a world away to pray through all 50 of these sin-soaked states of ours, because nobody here is capable to do that."

It made me wonder about when the tables are turned. What about the much more common scenario where we Americans travel around the world to do stuff the local people could do just as well, and probably do regularly? Like pray for their nation.

When someone comes here with best intentions to "save" us, I might even agree that we need saving, but it doesn't feel great to think that the visitors came because apparently they didn't trust that we could do the job ourselves. I found myself feeling a bit diminished as a representative of Christ in my culture, because in my mind the evangelist seemed to be passing judgment on our efficacy.

So, why should his people feel any differently when we come to his country with the same motives and messages to the local people? When we swoop in as eager saviors, how grateful should the recipients of our beneficence be?

I was quite busy today, so I kept doing other things and delaying my return phone call; it was easy to do. Then, as I swam laps after work, I remembered his call. And I remembered all the times I've traveled overseas and how colleagues or acquaintances or hosts dropped everything to come see me for an evening. The Americans I consider hospitable don't hold a candle to people in these other cultures, who spend money and time they can't afford to make visitors feel welcome. I knew how he'd treat my call if the tables were turned.

He's staying an hour away in Long Beach; if I call him now, it quite possibly means having to see him tonight, a two-hour round-trip drive and a total revision of my plans for the evening.

I remembered back to when we lived in Chicago and Janet and I came to California for a few days. We called an old high school friend who lived in Ventura. He and his wife jumped in the car that evening and drove an hour and a half each way to pick us up and take us out to dinner at their expense, to a place that was yet another half-hour away. (No, he's not a native Californian.)

What did I have to do this evening that was so important? I could bore you with my litany of priorities, which most Americans today would consider imminently reasonable but which most citizens in more hospitable cultures would likely label "lame excuses."

One of the nettlesome things about the lectionary, the Bible-reading calendar of the liturgical churches, is that you have to read through all the verses every few years. You don't get to skip over the pesky chapters. This past Sunday, the gospel reading was from Luke 11, where Jesus tells the parable of the man who pounds at your door after hours to borrow a loaf of bread (maybe today it would be a wine opener) because some friends just showed up unannounced, and you're already in bed and you turn over and yell at the door and tell him to take a flying leap. But finally, because he keeps asking, you get up and give it to him. Then Jesus says, continuing my paraphrase, "'If you who hardly care for your neighbor know how to give good gifts, how much more does your heavenly Father who loves you know how to be gracious to you?'"

There are times when it's no fun to remember a Scripture you heard at church, and this was definitely one of those times.

Maybe it was because by now I'd swum a mile and was feeling submissive. Or maybe it's because, once I'd turned the tables on my own reaction to my Indian friend's mission here, I could extend more grace back to him. In any case, I fought off my demons and just now returned his call. It was good to sense his warmth and kind heart on the phone. And thankfully, we arranged coffee for tomorrow before he flies to Honolulu, so I didn't have to get out of bed for the wine opener after all!

Today it was Hospitality - 1, Selfishness - 0.

Selfishness still has the insurmountable lead, but at least now it won't be a shutout. And I'm hoping maybe God grades on a curve after all.

Postscript: My Indian friend and I had a nice visit the next day, and the Lord even blessed me with an unexpected door prize for showing up, which alone made my effort more than worthwhile: At some point he mentioned Aylara community, the project which my dear donor friend Amy (now passed away) had underwritten, and which she and I had visited while in Kerala. "World Vision really should do a '25 years later' story on this community," he said. "We introduced rubber plants as an income-producing crop, and today there is no poverty there. All the children back then are now educated; the girls have been able to get jobs such as nurses. It's a wonderful success story!" It totally made my day, and now I remember why they say you can't out-give God.

Money Memories and Fears

So there I was, pinned down by a schoolmate, his fist ready to pound my face. I was totally clueless as to why he wanted to fight.

It happened 40 years ago. I don't think of it often, that embarrassing, puzzling memory from my brackish years in junior high. But when Suze Orman challenged readers in *The 9 Steps to Financial Freedom* to think of their most vivid childhood memory concerning money, I was stunned that this fight episode popped into my mind. And when she told readers to articulate their greatest money fear and then to find the link between the two, it finally made sense, all these decades later.

I was a young teen living on Bonforte Boulevard on a fashionable edge of Pueblo, Colorado. For the first time, our family had our own backyard pool. I attended an economically diverse school that included a number of Hispanic kids who lived in a poor immigrant area everyone simply called "Dogpatch" (if you can believe that hideous name). A Mexican slum on the edge of our little city of 100,000 souls.

In four years of living in Pueblo, I never went into Dogpatch. Nobody went there if they didn't need to. I hope to God it doesn't exist anymore.

But some of the kids from Dogpatch would become my sudden friends every summer during swimming season, and that was great. I don't think I ever really gave that too much thought; I harbored no cynical resentment. Anyway, they would take a shortcut through the prairie and hop onto our cinder-block wall to see what was up; and we'd all jump in the pool. Play is the great equalizer, at least on some level.

The Dogpatch kids would walk past my house to get to school too, though junior high is the great divider and we generally ran in different circles during the school year.

I was stunned when one of those hot-weather friends, David, wanted to fight me while walking home from school one day. I didn't want to fight him, but soon he was on top of me, his knees pinning my arms, his right fist quivering above my face. Pretending that the tear running into my ear was from "something in my eye," I asked him why he wanted to fight me. All he could say was that he didn't like my uppity attitude.

I realize now that David was probably frustrated at the disparity of our realities away from school, and that somehow I'd done something that seemed haughty or privileged to him and had painfully brought home the inequality of our opportunities. But what eighth-grade boy could express that in a moment of frustration and emotion? It'd be much simpler to just punch it out.

I had no idea that his gratitude for my summertime "charity" could turn into anger at the underlying injustice of a disparity neither of us had created, but in which we both played our roles.

But David never threw the punch. Mercy triumphed over retributive justice. We both went back to cordially playing our roles for the remaining months my family lived in Pueblo.

I never forgot the mystifying incident when I'd felt so vulnerable and clueless. As I've gotten older, I occasionally think of the episode and try to figure out another little piece of the puzzle.

It seemed odd to have that pop into my mind as a "money memory." But Suze's next challenge opened my eyes: Define your biggest fear regarding money (which at first I had trouble coming up with), and look for the almost-certain link between the early memory and the fear.

In that moment, I could suddenly name the fear. I saw the baggage.

My greatest money fear is simply this: living a life of ease in a sea of suffering. Swimming while others are drowning. Not caring.

Of course, the easy answer is to resist awareness, to create separate schools, separate areas, separate but unequal everything. This is, in fact, in large measure what we've done. And it's what I struggle with most about the lovely, homogeneously comfortable area where I now live.

You see, despite its risks, I worry that proximity may be my only hope for salvation from this. Just like the rich man in Jesus' story, who at least had an invalid beggar camped out at his gate. The rich man blew it in Jesus' simple parable (Luke 16:19-31). He ended up in hell, when caring for the poor beggar would seemingly have been his ticket to paradise.

But I don't even have the poor at my gates anymore to remind me of their reality. I've moved away, apart from those in need, and I've done so at my peril. Can I really understand and obey Jesus when I'm moving further from the things He would move closer to?

One Life

My colleague Cathi died yesterday. The news hit me hard. I feel sad and frustrated. For over a year, she'd searched and prayed for a bone marrow donor. I e-mailed her and found out we had similar ethnic backgrounds, which is supposedly somewhat important, so I offered to get my DNA typed. But I didn't want the hassle of going to the right hospital an hour away, so I stalled for two months waiting for a convenient moment, which never came. Eventually I took the time to get it done, but I received no results for four more months. I finally phoned for them three weeks ago. I e-mailed Cathi that I now had my data, but I never received a reply. Ever. I've just now called the marrow hotline: They assured me that my data would have already been on their website and checked every day for a match. So quite likely I wasn't her type.

Or maybe she was too sick by then to warrant a donor.

And therein lies the issue: I moved slowly, at my own comfortable speed, as a healthy person who was trying to be nice to an acquaintance but for whom this was simply a hassle. Meanwhile, for Cathi, it was life itself. When we e-mailed about various work-related topics, she always encouraged me to get tested; yet she never pressured me or complained at my slowness. Frankly, I just wanted someone else to solve this, someone else who wouldn't be so put out by the time and money involved, or who wouldn't care about being put out, anyway. I was busy saving people. I had too little time to save just one person.

I hear a drumbeat of shame; I fell into the trap I see so many others fall into, and for which I often judge them: "This doesn't impact me personally, so I'm only going to care when I can conveniently spare the time and money."

"'Who is my neighbor?'" Jesus was asked (Luke 10:29). The ones it's convenient to help?

I ask you to forgive me, Lord, and help me forgive myself. Help me to be more merciful toward others who do the same things. May I see in their sins of omission my own sins of omission and self-centeredness, and repent, rather than condemn.

You see, only two hours before getting the news about Cathi, I'd read a magazine article, "Three Pounds Too Late," about a 4-year-old girl named Faith who was dying of AIDS. She no longer qualified to receive the precious drugs that could save her life, because by the time they were available she was 3 pounds too frail. The author's understanding of the global AIDS crisis was transformed in an instant through this singular person, this docile little girl wearing a ragged, second-hand party dress. Faith's life and tragedy changed the writer's view of her own life, her priorities, and her urgencies; she now saw spiritual formation as "being conformed to the image of Christ for the sake of others." And she declared that no one should ever again be "3 pounds too late" because of apathy on the part of those who don't make the effort to know or care. But it was too late for Faith.

That evening, it dawned on me: I, personally, was three months too late for Cathi. Not due to apathy (I could never shake the feeling that I should get myself typed), but rather to lethargy. The lethargy of the comfortable, the unaffected. And, regardless of the label for it, the impact for Cathi was the same.

It only takes one story—one life—to inspire caring. "A million deaths is a statistic; one death is a tragedy," said Stalin, who would know. The death of Faith, one little girl, ignited an author's compassion for millions more impacted by HIV and AIDS.

Ultimately, caring plays out one person at a time, too. Somewhere down the line from my relatively comfortable perch at World Vision, on this side of the caring equation, the desire and the funds to care for many in need trickle down to one individual person in need, one singular act of compassion, one at a time. "Everyone" becomes "this one." Cathi was one. Just one.

"One life!" shout kids from around the globe on a fast-paced World Vision video. For three minutes, face after face appears in sequence, each in his or her own accent and setting, holding up a single finger, reminding the viewer, "You have one life!" Near the end the theme changes just slightly: "I have one life." Each time I watch, I have to catch the sudden sob that surprises me as child after child, full of life and potential, declares their one fragile shot on this planet.

The power of one, of one life impacting one life. The preciousness of her one story, his one story, my one story, rises to a crescendo in the video's final cry:

"I have only one life. Won't you do something?"

Drinking Deeply

My Los Angeles counterpart, Jeff, phoned me to check in while he was in East Africa on a Vision Trip with a donor couple. It was 3 a.m. there and he was having trouble sleeping.

Jeff told me that earlier that day the group had visited a remote community where women and children had to walk several miles just to collect polluted water. His small band of visitors made the pilgrimage to the water hole along with the community members and their donkeys. The journey ended at a 3-foot-deep hole dug adjacent to a dirty pool of standing water. Inside the hole, a 40-something woman squatted, scooping brown water by the quart as it sifted through the sandy soil and refilled a little divot. The centuries-old sand was their only filter for whatever maladies lurked in the pond water (in which those same donkeys stand and drink).

As I listened, I instantly remembered making a similar trek two decades ago in northern Kenya, walking to the water hole dug into a dry riverbed, watching the children scoop the murky brown liquid. I'm ashamed to admit that I mainly recalled the experience as an adventure. I remembered the fascination of the trek, not the angst I felt when I realized how desperately these people lived every day, hoping the little divot in the riverbed would fill with groundwater so they could scoop water sufficient for the day into a dirty jerrycan.

A minute later, I asked Jeff about their journey to Africa. He said they'd spent a transit night in Dubai, where the donor arranged for them all to enjoy a lovely dinner at the top of a hotel famous for offering the most expensive drink in the world—at $9,000. Then, just 48 hours after he'd been with people who sell a $9,000 cocktail, Jeff spent the day with desperate people in an area where water good enough to drink isn't available at any price.

The disparities in this world aren't usually that stark, but the story points to a reality we all try to make sense of. This is our challenge as we journey through life, those of us who can move freely between the worlds of the least-haves and the most-haves. We're surrounded hourly by temporal temptations and little luxuries, hearing the constant messages that we deserve more—messages that almost drown out the distant realities and feeble petitions from "the rest of these," our brethren.

When we do hear and try to respond, we face the temptation to turn even our God-ordained encounters with the poor into personal adventure stories. "I braved Darfur." "I conquered the Amazon." "I saved a sick Ethiopian woman," we declare on our internal memory drives, if not on our souvenir t-shirts.

How much we need each other's companionship and confessions on this journey. For we are pilgrims, uncertainly attempting to walk the Jesus Road. As those with the audacity to at least try to hear and obey Jesus' voice—His radical call—we are called to make pilgrimages, to travel strange roads to distant lands toward His voice. Yet in the back of our minds we sometimes wonder if we're really walking His road or traveling another path.

The journey is arduous. Let's admit it: Opening one's eyes and heart to the poor is ultimately a voluntary exercise for those of us who aren't forced to live that reality. Yet, though it's far more taxing than moutaineering, we sense that the road will climb to the Promised Land, a place of deep satisfaction and true freedom. Freedom from what possesses us.

Along the road, we are refreshed. When we follow Jesus' example of active compassion for the poor and dispossessed, we find the experience is holy, slaking a deep thirst in us as much as in them.

Holy, like pure, blessed water seeping into a divot, waiting to be scooped and drunk deeply by all of us circled round—all of us, together.

I love the pilgrimage. If I hunt with the eyes of my heart along the journey, I may return bearing treasures from afar.

Afterword

Coming Back from Afar, Bearing Gifts

A stranger gave me a wonderful gift the other day. We were both attending a training seminar on how to help people tap into their philanthropic passions. The trainer predicted, "Every time a class does this next exercise, several attendees have an epiphany."

It was a two-person role-play, except that as the responder, I was to simply be myself. My role-play partner, whom I'd just met, dutifully asked me, "What would you like to do with your money that would be meaningful to you?" No surprise: I talked about helping the global poor, especially children.

"Tell me more."

"Well, I've always had an interest in poverty, I suppose. I did the 'trick or treat for UNICEF' thing for many years as a child. And I volunteered at an inner-city hospital for two summers in high school in Kansas City." I rattled off a few additional examples.

She honed in and asked how I ever decided to volunteer at an inner-city hospital—me, a white kid from the suburbs. And I couldn't remember. I really had no clue. I don't think I'd ever thought about it.

Then I remembered my junior high encounter with David, the boy from Dogpatch, which had happened the summer before we moved to Kansas City. I began volunteering the very next summer.

Suddenly, the pieces came together for me. Less than a year after I was jumped by this angry kid, my life's trajectory was changing. I came to the shocking realization of the existence of "others," and knew that I didn't really have the foggiest notion of how the "others" lived. Somehow that moved me to do something to cross the divide that separated us.

I started to exclaim, "Why, this explains … " My role-play partner interrupted me, "… your whole life!"

I shared a holy moment of personal discovery with a near-total stranger, and we both sensed the powerful gift of understanding I'd been given. Coming to the realization that there were "others," people who didn't live as I lived and didn't think as I thought, somehow made me realize how much I needed to listen, and to learn. Amazingly, the trauma that led to this discovery hadn't scared me away; it became an invitation, a door that gradually opened onto a new pathway for my life. The reality that there were fellow human beings "afar off" (though I shared the same ZIP code with some of them) became an invitation to draw near.

God has continued to open additional doors leading me further along the way, and the journey of discovery has been remarkable.

Like that junior high encounter, something usually prompts the journey, just as something prompted you to read this book and take this journey. Whatever the prodding is for you, it's an invitation from your heart.

I hope you'll accept that invitation and stay the course, letting every person be your teacher, even the least and the last. Maybe especially the least and the last, the unknown "others." As Mother Teresa reminded us, there we will encounter Jesus, in the distressing disguise of the poor. Distressing perhaps; yet this is also where kingdom treasure lies.

The magi, those wise men from the Christmas story, bore gifts. Those who are afar often have gifts for us too, whether afar is across the ocean or across the tracks. When we return home with such gifts, we will glimpse more clearly how God sees our world, and our place in it.

About World Vision

World Vision is a Christian humanitarian organization dedicated to working with children, families, and their communities worldwide to reach their full potential by tackling the causes of poverty and injustice. Motivated by our faith in Jesus Christ, World Vision serves alongside the poor and oppressed as a demonstration of God's unconditional love for all people.

We envision a world where each child experiences "fullness of life" as described in John 10:10. We know this can be achieved only by addressing the problems of poverty and injustice in a holistic way. World Vision brings 60 years of experience in three key areas to help children and families thrive: emergency relief, long-term development, and advocacy. We bring our skills across many areas of expertise to each community where we work, enabling us to support children's physical, social, emotional, and spiritual well-being.

Partnering with World Vision provides tangible ways to honor God and put faith into action. By working together, we can make a lasting difference in the lives of children and families who are struggling to overcome poverty. To find out more about how you can help, visit **www.worldvision.org**.

About World Vision Resources

Ending global poverty and injustice begins with education: understanding the magnitude and causes of poverty, its impact on human dignity, and our connection to those in need around the world.

World Vision Resources is the publishing ministry of World Vision, educating Christians about global poverty, inspiring them to respond, and equipping them with innovative resources to make a difference in the world.

For more information, contact:

World Vision Resources
Mail Stop 321
P.O. Box 9716
Federal Way, WA 98063-9716
Fax: 253.815.3340
wvresources@worldvision.org
www.worldvisionresources.org